THE COMPLETE
Cajun Vegan
COOKBOOK

KELLI J.
DOCTOR

Flavorful Plant-Based Recipes
Inspired by Cajun Cuisine

TABLE OF CONTENT

INTRODUCTION

Embark on a gastronomic adventure with "The Complete Cajun Vegan Cookbook" as we explore the plant-based world while preserving the robust flavors of Cajun food. This cookbook is an ode to the rich culinary history of Louisiana through recreated classic Cajun meals made with colorful, cruelty-free ingredients.

The rich flavors of Cajun cuisine are the result of a fusion of several civilizations, including those of the French, the Spanish, the Africans, and the Native Americans. While traditional Cajun fare has focused on seafood, pork, and hearty stews, we aim to prove that plant-based alternatives can taste just as rich and fulfilling without sacrificing any of the authentic flavors that have made this cuisine so popular.

Anyone from a seasoned vegan seeking new recipes to try to a Cajun foodie interested in trying vegan alternatives will find something to their liking in this booklet. We have painstakingly created every recipe—from savoury étouffée and crunchy okra to spicy jambalaya and gumbo—to convey the spirit of Cajun food while adhering to the ideals of veganism.

Along with the delectable recipes, you'll discover practical advice on how to cook with different ingredients, different methods, and how to replicate the special spices that make Cajun cuisine unique. Vegan Cajun cuisine is full of innovative flavors and textures, so we hope you'll approach it with an open mind and a hunger for adventure.

Get your apron on, round up your ingredients, and set off on a vegan culinary expedition that honors the soul of Cajun cuisine. "The Complete Cajun Vegan Cookbook" is going to be a unique and tasty addition to your kitchen with its hearty recipes and spicy, flavorful foods.

BASICS OF THE COMPLETE CAJUN VEGAN COOKBOOK:

Essential Cajun Flavors:

Immerse yourself in the soul of Cajun cooking by learning its signature tastes. The dishes are a culinary symphony that honors their cultural origins, with flavors ranging from the holy trinity of celery, onion, and bell pepper to powerful spices like paprika, cayenne, and thyme.

Plant-Based Swaps:

Learning how to make delicious vegan versions of classic Cajun foods is an art form. Get the lowdown on how to make meatless meat alternatives like tempeh, tofu, or seitan taste just as good as the real thing. Discover the plethora of vegetables that can enhance the flavor and texture of your dishes.

Cajun Pantry Staples:

Invest on a few key Cajun ingredients to take your vegan recipes to the next level. Along your journey into vegan Cajun cuisine, you will learn to rely on four essentials: gumbo file powder, liquid smoke, okra, and grits.

TIPS AND TRICKS:

Mastering Spice Levels:

The robust and fiery tastes are what make Cajun food so famous. Master the art of balancing heat with other flavors and modify the amount of spice to your liking. Make your own Cajun seasoning blends by experimenting with different homemade spice mixes.

Slow Cooking Magic:

Embrace the method of slow cooking that is characteristic of traditional Cajun cuisine. Over time, flavors can combine and become even more intense, transforming ordinary ingredients into exquisite culinary works of art. To get the real Cajun flavor and texture, get a high-quality Dutch oven or slow cooker.

Fresh and Local Ingredients:

Fresh, locally grown produce should be sourced wherever possible. Vegan Cajun dishes will taste even better and be more authentic if you use fresh, seasonal ingredients, since high-quality ingredients are the foundation of Cajun cooking.

Interactive Cooking Experience:

The method is just as important as the product when it comes to Cajun cooking. Gather around the stove and let your loved ones help you out. Bring each other joy by making healthy, plant-based Cajun dishes while sharing tales and laughs.

With the help of "The Complete Cajun Vegan Cookbook," a vegan can enjoy all the flavorful, spicy goodness of authentic Cajun food without sacrificing any of the plant-based ingredients. This guidebook will take you on a culinary adventure where plant-based and Cajun flavors meld in the most delicious way, whether you're making a hearty gumbo or enjoying jambalaya. The distinctive culinary tradition is defined by bright and soul-satisfying delicacies, so get ready to enjoy.

1. DIRTY RICE-STUFFED PATTYPAN SQUASH

Total Time: 1 hour 30 minutes

Prep Time: 30 minutes

Ingredients:

- 6 pattypan squash
- 1 cup brown rice, cooked
- 1 cup vegan ground sausage
- 1 onion, finely chopped
- 1 bell pepper, diced
- 2 celery stalks, finely chopped
- 3 cloves garlic, minced
- 1 teaspoon Cajun seasoning
- Salt and pepper to taste
- 2 tablespoons vegetable oil
- 1 cup vegetable broth
- Chopped green onions for garnish

Directions:

1. Bring the oven temperature up to 375 °F or 190 °C.
2. Remove the seeds from the pattypan squash by first removing the tops of the squash.
3. Prepare the vegetable oil by heating it in a pan over medium heat. When the onion, bell pepper, celery, and garlic have become more tender, sauté them.
4. Cajun seasoning, vegan ground sausage, salt, and pepper should be added to the stew. Ensure that the sausage is browned by cooking it.
5. The cooked rice and veggie broth should be stirred in. Simmer until the broth is completely absorbed.
6. The rice mixture should be stuffed into each pattypan squash, and then the squash should be placed in a baking dish.
7. Place the foil on top, and bake for forty-five minutes. Take the lid off after 15 minutes and bake the squash for another 15–20 minutes or until it's cooked through to your liking.
8. Prior to serving, garnish with green onions that have been chopped.

2. CREOLE ROASTED BRUSSELS SPROUTS

Total Time: 40 minutes

Prep Time: 10 minutes

Ingredients:

- 1 lb Brussels sprouts, trimmed and halved
- 2 tablespoons olive oil
- 2 tablespoons Creole seasoning
- 1 tablespoon maple syrup
- Salt and pepper to taste
- Lemon wedges for serving

Directions:

1. Roast the vegetables until they are soft, about 20 minutes before serving.
2. Olive oil, Creole seasoning, maple syrup, salt, and pepper should be mixed together in a dish and then tossed with Brussels sprouts.
3. Position the Brussels sprouts in a single layer on a baking sheet and set it in the oven.
4. Until brown and crispy, roast for twenty-five to thirty minutes, rotating once halfway through.
5. It is recommended to serve lemon wedges on the side.

3. VEGAN ANDOUILLE SAUSAGE GRITS

Total Time: 45 minutes

Prep Time: 15 minutes

Ingredients:

- 1 cup stone-ground grits
- 4 cups vegetable broth
- 1 cup unsweetened almond milk
- 1 cup vegan Andouille sausage, sliced
- 1 onion, finely chopped
- 1 bell pepper, diced
- 3 cloves garlic, minced
- 2 tablespoons nutritional yeast
- Salt and pepper to taste
- Fresh parsley for garnish

Directions:

1. Both the vegetable broth and the almond milk should be brought to a boil in a pot. Take the skillet from the stove and mix in the grits.
2. Simmer, stirring the mixture regularly, until it has thickened.
3. Stir-frying vegan Andouille sausage, onion, bell pepper, and garlic in a pan until the veggies are cooked is the recommended method.
4. Combine the sausage mixture with the grits that have been cooked before adding the nutritional yeast, pepper, and salt, and mix until combined.
5. Add five more minutes of cooking time until the flavors have merged.
6. Immediately prior to serving, garnish with fresh parsley.

4. SPICY OKRA AND TOMATO GRITS

Total Time: 50 minutes

Prep Time: 20 minutes

Ingredients:

- 1 cup stone-ground grits
- 4 cups vegetable broth
- 2 cups fresh okra, sliced
- 1 can (14 oz) diced tomatoes, drained
- 1 onion, finely chopped

- 3 cloves garlic, minced
- 1 teaspoon Cajun seasoning
- 1/2 teaspoon red pepper flakes
- Salt and pepper to taste
- Chopped green onions for garnish

Directions:

1. Using vegetable broth, prepare grits in accordance with the directions provided on the box.
2. Onion, garlic, and okra should be sautéed together in a pan until the okra is just beginning to brown.
3. Tomatoes that have been diced, Cajun spice, crushed red pepper, salt, and pepper should be added. Continue to cook until the food is completely heated.
4. Incorporate the okra-tomato combination into the grits that have been cooked. Give it a good stir.
5. The flavors should be allowed to combine for a further ten minutes of cooking.
6. Prior to serving, garnish with green onions that have been chopped.

5. BLACKENED TEMPEH CAESAR SALAD

Total Time: 30 minutes

Prep Time: 15 minutes

Ingredients:

- 1 package of tempeh, sliced
- 2 tablespoons Cajun seasoning
- 1 tablespoon olive oil
- 1 head of romaine lettuce, chopped
- 1 cup cherry tomatoes, halved
- 1/2 cup croutons (check for vegan options)
- 1/4 cup vegan Caesar dressing
- Salt and pepper to taste

Directions:

1. Cajun seasoning should be tossed with tempeh slices in a bowl, making sure that the coating is equal.
2. Get the olive oil heated up to medium-high in a skillet.
3. Cook the tempeh slices until they are browned on both sides, which should take around three to four minutes on each side.
4. The romaine lettuce, cherry tomatoes, croutons, and tempeh that have been blackened should be mixed together in a big salad dish.
5. Once the vegan Caesar dressing has been drizzled over the salad, toss it until it is well incorporated.
6. Before seasoning with salt, add pepper and salt to taste. Provide prompt service.

6. DIRTY CAULIFLOWER RICE AND BLACK BEANS

Total Time: 40 minutes

Prep Time: 15 minutes

Ingredients:

- 1 medium cauliflower, grated
- 1 can black beans, drained and rinsed
- 1 bell pepper, diced
- 1 onion, finely chopped
- 3 cloves garlic, minced
- 2 tablespoons Cajun seasoning
- 1 tablespoon olive oil
- Green onions for garnish
- Salt and pepper to taste

Directions:

1. In a big pan over medium heat, prepare the olive oil.
2. Sauté the onions, garlic, and bell pepper until they have attained a softened state.
3. When the cauliflower has been grated, add it to the pan and toss in the Cajun spice. Bake for ten to twelve minutes, stirring the mixture regularly.
4. To finish heating the black beans, stir them in and continue cooking.
5. Before seasoning with salt, add pepper and salt to taste. Prior to serving, garnish with green onions that have been chopped.

7. CAJUN-STYLE VEGAN MASHED POTATOES

Total Time: 45 minutes

Prep Time: 20 minutes

Ingredients:

- 4 large potatoes, peeled and diced
- 1/2 cup unsweetened almond milk
- 2 tablespoons vegan butter
- 2 teaspoons Cajun seasoning
- Salt and pepper to taste
- Chopped chives for garnish

Directions:

1. To make the potatoes tender with a fork, boil them in water. After draining, place the contents back into the pot.
2. You should mash the potatoes and then add the Cajun spice, vegan butter, almond milk, and salt and pepper to taste. Continue mashing until no lumps remain.
3. Add more almond milk to modify the consistency if needed. Taste, then make any necessary adjustments to the seasoning.
4. Add some chopped chives as a garnish, and serve the dish hot.

8. JAZZY JACKFRUIT AND BLACK BEAN QUESADILLAS

Total Time: 35 minutes

Prep Time: 20 minutes

Ingredients:

- 1 can young jackfruit, shredded
- 1 can black beans, drained and rinsed
- 1 onion, finely chopped
- 2 cloves garlic, minced
- 2 tablespoons Cajun seasoning

- 1 teaspoon smoked paprika
- 4 large tortillas
- Vegan cheese, shredded
- Fresh cilantro, chopped
- Salsa and guacamole for serving

Directions:

1. In a pan, sauté the garlic and onions until they are more soft. Jackfruit that has been shredded, black beans, Cajun spice, and smoky paprika should be added. For ten to twelve minutes, cook.
2. Place the tortillas on the table, and on half of each tortilla, put a layer of the jackfruit and black bean mixture.
3. The topping should be topped with vegan cheese and fresh cilantro. The tortillas should be folded in half.
4. Prepare a skillet that does not stick by heating it over medium heat. On each side, cook each quesadilla for two to three minutes until it reaches a golden brown color.
5. Cut it into slices and serve it with guacamole and salsa.

9. CREOLE STUFFED ZUCCHINI BOATS

Total Time: 45 minutes

Prep Time: 15 minutes

Ingredients:

- 4 medium zucchini
- 1 cup cooked quinoa
- 1 can (15 oz) black beans, drained and rinsed
- 1 cup diced tomatoes
- 1 cup diced bell peppers (assorted colors)
- 1 cup diced onions
- 2 cloves garlic, minced
- 1 tablespoon Cajun seasoning
- Salt and pepper to taste
- 2 tablespoons olive oil
- Fresh parsley for garnish

Directions:

1. Bring the oven temperature up to 375 °F or 190 °C. On each zucchini, cut it in half along its length. Using a spoon, remove the seeds, therefore forming a hollow "boat."
2. The quinoa, black beans, tomatoes, bell peppers, onions, garlic, Cajun spice, salt, and pepper should be mixed together with the individual ingredients in a large mixing basin. Combine thoroughly.
3. Place a little of the quinoa mixture inside of each zucchini boat.
4. The zucchini that has been filled should be placed on a baking dish and drizzled with olive oil.
5. For twenty-five to thirty minutes, or until the zucchini is soft, bake it.
6. When serving, sprinkle freshly chopped parsley over top and serve hot.

10.   VEGAN BREAD PUDDING WITH WHISKEY SAUCE

Total Time: 1 hour

Prep Time: 15 minutes

Ingredients:

- 6 cups cubed day-old French bread
- 2 cups almond milk
- 1 cup sugar
- 1/2 cup melted coconut oil
- 1 tablespoon ground flaxseeds
- 1 teaspoon vanilla extract
- 1/2 teaspoon ground cinnamon
- 1/4 teaspoon ground nutmeg
- Pinch of salt
- Whiskey Sauce:
- 1/2 cup coconut cream
- 1/4 cup brown sugar
- 2 tablespoons vegan whiskey

Directions:

1. Set the oven's temperature to 175 degrees Celsius, or 350 degrees F.
2. The bread cubes, almond milk, sugar, coconut oil, flaxseeds, vanilla essence, cinnamon, nutmeg, and a bit of salt should be mixed together in a big bowl containing all of the ingredients. Combine thoroughly.
3. Place the mixture in a baking dish that has been buttered and bake it for forty to forty-five minutes or until it is brown and set.
4. While the pudding is in the oven, you can make the whiskey sauce by bringing the brown sugar and coconut cream together in a pot and heating them over medium heat. Whisky should be added after the sugar has been stirred until it has dissolved. Maintain a low simmer for five minutes.
5. Before serving, pour the whiskey sauce over the bread pudding that has been prepared.

11.   QUINOA JAMBALAYA STUFFED PEPPERS

Total Time: 40 minutes

Prep Time: 20 minutes

Ingredients:

- 4 large bell peppers, halved and seeds removed
- 1 cup cooked quinoa
- 1 cup diced tomatoes
- 1 cup black-eyed peas, cooked
- 1 cup diced celery
- 1 cup diced onions
- 2 cloves garlic, minced
- 1 teaspoon Cajun seasoning
- 1/2 teaspoon paprika
- Salt and pepper to taste
- 2 tablespoons olive oil
- Green onions for garnish

Directions:

1. Bring the oven temperature up to 375 °F or 190 °C. All of the ingredients, including quinoa, tomatoes, black-eyed peas, celery, onions, garlic, Cajun spice, paprika, salt, and pepper, should be mixed together in a large mixing basin. Combine thoroughly.
2. Place a little of the quinoa mixture inside of each pepper half.
3. Arrange the packed peppers on a baking dish, drizzle with olive oil, and tent them with aluminum foil.
4. Bake the peppers for twenty to twenty-five minutes or until they are soft.
5. Prior to serving, garnish with green onions that have been chopped.

12.   SMOKY OKRA AND TOMATO SALAD

Total Time: 20 minutes

Prep Time: 10 minutes

Ingredients:

- 1 pound fresh okra, trimmed and halved
- 1 cup cherry tomatoes, halved
- 1 red onion, finely sliced
- 2 cloves garlic, minced
- 2 tablespoons olive oil
- 1 teaspoon smoked paprika
- 1 teaspoon cumin
- Salt and pepper to taste
- 2 tablespoons fresh parsley, chopped (for garnish)

Directions:

1. Put the okra that has been cut in half, the cherry tomatoes, and the red onion that has been sliced into a large mixing bowl.
2. Gather all of the dressing ingredients in a small bowl and mix them together. Add the minced garlic, olive oil, smoked paprika, cumin, salt, and pepper.
3. Drizzle the dressing over the tomato and okra combination that has been prepared. Gently toss the ingredients together to ensure that they are evenly covered.
4. A skillet should be heated over medium heat. Combine the okra that has been prepared with the tomatoes in the skillet and sauté them for eight to ten minutes, or until the okra is soft but still has a tiny crunch to it.
5. Remove the salad from the heat and place it on a dish that is suitable for serving. Garnish with fresh parsley that has been chopped.
6. The meal may be served immediately as a savory side dish, or it can be allowed to gradually cool down and then served at room temperature.

13.   CAJUN LENTIL SOUP

Total Time: 1 hour 30 minutes

Prep Time: 15 minutes

Servings: 4

Ingredients:

- 1 cup dried green lentils, rinsed and drained
- 1 onion, finely chopped
- 2 celery stalks, diced
- 2 carrots, peeled and sliced
- 3 cloves garlic, minced
- 1 can (14 oz) diced tomatoes

- 6 cups vegetable broth
- 1 teaspoon Cajun seasoning
- 1/2 teaspoon smoked paprika
- Salt and pepper to taste
- 2 bay leaves
- 2 cups kale, chopped
- Fresh parsley for garnish

Directions:

1. The onion, celery, and carrots should be sautéed in a large saucepan over medium heat until they have become more tender.
2. The following ingredients should be added: garlic, lentils, chopped tomatoes, vegetable broth, Cajun spice, smoked paprika, salt, pepper, and bay leaves. Assume a boiling point.
3. Reduce the heat, cover, and simmer the lentils for forty-five to fifty minutes or until they are soft.
4. The greens should be stirred in and cooked for a further ten minutes.
5. To serve, remove the bay leaves, make any necessary adjustments to the seasoning, and top with fresh parsley.

14.   DIRTY RICE-STUFFED ACORN SQUASH RINGS

Total Time: 1 hour 15 minutes

Prep Time: 20 minutes

Servings: 6

Ingredients:

- 3 acorn squash, cut into rings and seeds removed
- 1 cup brown rice, cooked
- 1 lb vegan ground sausage
- 1 onion, diced
- 1 bell pepper, diced
- 3 celery stalks, diced
- 3 cloves garlic, minced
- 1 tablespoon Cajun seasoning
- Salt and pepper to taste
- 2 green onions, chopped for garnish

Directions:

1. Bring the oven temperature up to 375 °F or 190 °C. Roast the acorn squash rings on a baking sheet for thirty to thirty-five minutes or until they are soft when pierced with a fork.
2. The vegan sausage, onion, bell pepper, and celery should be cooked in a large pan until the veggies are soft.
3. Garlic, rice that has been cooked, Cajun spice, salt, and pepper should be added. Give it a good stir.
4. Place a portion of the dirty rice mixture inside each ring of acorn squash.
5. You should continue baking for another 15–20 minutes.
6. Prior to serving, garnish with green onions that have been chopped.

15.   VEGAN MIRLITON CASSEROLE

Total Time: 1 hour 15 minutes

Prep Time: 25 minutes

Servings: 8

Ingredients:

- 4 mirlitons (chayotes), peeled, seeded, and diced
- 1 cup diced tomatoes
- 1 onion, finely chopped
- 1 bell pepper, diced
- 3 cloves garlic, minced
- 1 cup corn kernels
- oil
- 1 cup black beans, cooked
- 1/2 cup vegetable broth
- 2 teaspoons Cajun seasoning
- 1 teaspoon thyme
- Salt and pepper to taste
- 1 cup breadcrumbs
- 2 tablespoons olive

Directions:

1. Bring the oven up to a temperature of 375 F (190 C).
2. Mirlitons that have been diced should be boiled until they are soft, which should take around 15 minutes. Drain, then keep away for later use.
3. To soften the onion, bell pepper, and garlic, sauté them in a large pan until they are tender.
4. Cajun seasoning, diced tomatoes, corn, black beans, vegetable broth, thyme, salt, and pepper should be added to the mixture. 5-7 minutes of cooking time.
5. Stir in the mirlitons that have been cooked, then transfer to a casserole dish.
6. The breadcrumbs and olive oil should be mixed together in a small basin. Scatter the toppings over the dish.
7. Cook for twenty-five to thirty minutes or until the top is a golden brown color.

16.   CAJUN CORN AND POTATO SALAD

Total Time: 45 minutes

Prep Time: 15 minutes

Servings: 6

Ingredients:

- 4 cups baby potatoes, boiled and quartered
- 2 cups corn kernels, cooked
- 1 red bell pepper, diced
- 1/2 cup red onion, finely chopped
- 1/4 cup fresh parsley, chopped
- 1/4 cup vegan mayonnaise
- 2 tablespoons Dijon mustard
- 1 tablespoon Cajun seasoning
- Salt and pepper to taste
- Lemon wedges for serving

Directions:

1. Gather the potatoes, corn, red bell pepper, red onion, and parsley into a big basin and mix them together.
2. By mixing all of the ingredients together in a small bowl, you can combine vegan mayonnaise, Dijon mustard, Cajun spice, salt, and pepper until everything is well combined.
3. Once the dressing has been poured over the potato mixture, toss it until it is evenly covered.
4. Maintain in the refrigerator for at least half an hour before serving.
5. The dish should be served with lemon wedges and garnished with more parsley.

17.   CAJUN CORN AND BLACK BEAN SALAD

Total Time: 15 minutes

Prep Time: 10 minutes

Ingredients:

- 1 can (15 oz) black beans, drained and rinsed
- 1 cup corn kernels (fresh or frozen, thawed)
- 1 cup cherry tomatoes, halved
- 1/2 red onion, finely chopped
- 1/4 cup fresh cilantro, chopped
- 1 avocado, diced
- 2 tablespoons olive oil
- 2 tablespoons lime juice
- 1 teaspoon Cajun seasoning
- Salt and pepper to taste

Directions:

1. A big bowl should be used to incorporate the following Ingredients: black beans, corn, cherry tomatoes, red onion, cilantro, and avocado.
2. If you want to make the Cajun spice, put the lime juice, salt, pepper, and olive oil into a small dish and mix them together. Combine thoroughly. Have fun!
3. After pouring the dressing over the salad, carefully mix it to blend the ingredients.
4. Before serving, allow the dish to chill in the refrigerator for at least half an hour.
5. Use this recipe as a refreshing side dish or main dish, and garnish it with more cilantro (optional).

18.   CAJUN STUFFED BELL PEPPERS

Total Time: 1 hour

Prep Time: 20 minutes

Ingredients:

- 4 large bell peppers, halved and seeds removed
- 1 cup quinoa, cooked
- 1 can (15 oz) black beans, drained and rinsed
- 1 cup corn kernels (fresh or frozen, thawed)
- 1 cup diced tomatoes
- 1 cup diced zucchini
- 1/2 cup diced red onion
- 2 cloves garlic, minced
- 2 teaspoons Cajun seasoning
- 1 cup tomato sauce
- Salt and pepper to taste
- 1 cup vegan cheese, shredded (optional)

Directions:

1. Bring the oven temperature up to 375 °F or 190 °C. The quinoa, black beans, corn, tomatoes, zucchini, red onion, garlic, Cajun spice, salt, and pepper should be mixed together in a big bowl along with the other ingredients.
2. After stuffing each half of the bell pepper with the quinoa mixture, put the peppers in a ceramic baking dish.
3. After the peppers have been filled, cover the dish with aluminum foil and pour tomato sauce over the peppers.
4. After forty minutes in the oven, remove the dish from the oven and, if preferred, sprinkle vegan cheese on top.
5. For a further fifteen to twenty minutes, or until the peppers are soft, continue baking.
6. Be sure to serve this tasty Cajun meal while it is still hot!

19.   CAJUN BLACK BEAN AND CORN SALSA

Total Time: 20 minutes

Prep Time: 15 minutes

Ingredients:

- 1 can (15 oz) black beans, drained and rinsed
- 1 cup corn kernels (fresh or frozen, thawed)
- 1 cup diced tomatoes
- 1/2 cup red bell pepper, finely chopped
- 1/4 cup red onion, finely chopped
- 1/4 cup fresh cilantro, chopped
- 2 tablespoons lime juice
- 1 tablespoon olive oil
- 1 teaspoon Cajun seasoning
- Salt and pepper to taste

Directions:

1. The black beans, corn, tomatoes, red bell pepper, red onion, and cilantro should be mixed together in a large bowl by the cook.
2. It is recommended to combine lime juice, olive oil, Cajun spice, salt, and pepper in a small bowl and mix them together.
3. To blend the salsa and dressing, pour the dressing over the salsa and gently toss.
4. To enable the flavors to combine, place the dish in the refrigerator for at least half an hour.
5. Take pleasure in the Cajun flavor that is present in each and every mouthful by serving it with tortilla chips or as a topping for tacos.

20.   VEGAN ANDOUILLE SAUSAGE SLIDERS

Total Time: 45 minutes

Prep Time: 20 minutes

Ingredients:

- 1 package (12 oz) vegan Andouille sausages, sliced
- 1 tablespoon olive oil
- 1 onion, thinly sliced
- 1 bell pepper, thinly sliced
- 1 teaspoon Cajun seasoning
- 1/2 teaspoon smoked paprika
- Salt and pepper to taste
- Slider buns
- Vegan coleslaw for topping (optional)

Directions:

1. In a big pan over medium heat, prepare the olive oil.
2. Stir in some sliced Andouille sausages, along with some onion and bell pepper, to the skillet.
3. Cajun spice, smoked paprika, salt, and pepper should be used to season the dish. The sausages should be browned, and the veggies should be cooked until they are soft.
4. You can either use a pan or the oven to toast slider buns.
5. Place a liberal amount of the Andouille mixture on each bun, and then proceed to assemble the sliders.
6. If desired, vegan coleslaw can be placed on top.
7. Serve these sliders with a Cajun influence while they are still warm.

21.   BLACKENED TOFU AND CORN GRITS

Total Time: 40 minutes

Prep Time: 15 minutes

Ingredients:

- 1 block of firm tofu, pressed and sliced
- 1 cup corn grits
- 2 tablespoons Cajun seasoning
- 1 teaspoon smoked paprika
- 1 tablespoon olive oil
- Salt and pepper to taste
- Fresh parsley for garnish

Directions:

1. Cook the corn grits in accordance with the directions on the box.
2. Mix the Cajun spice, smoked paprika, salt, and pepper together in a bowl. Cajun spice is found in the Louisiana region.
3. The spice combination should be rubbed over the tofu slices in order to ensure that it is spread uniformly throughout the tofu products.
4. The olive oil should be brought to a simmer in a skillet that is set over medium-high heat.
5. To get a blackened appearance, cook tofu slices for three to four minutes on each side.
6. On top of a bed of corn grits, serve tofu that has been charred.
7. Enjoy this dish with some fresh parsley as a garnish!

22.   SWEET POTATO GRITS WITH CAJUN SPINACH

Total Time: 45 minutes

Prep Time: 20 minutes

Ingredients:

- 1 cup sweet potato, grated
- 1 cup corn grits
- 2 cups fresh spinach
- 1 onion, finely chopped
- 3 cloves garlic, minced

- 1 tablespoon Cajun seasoning
- 2 tablespoons nutritional yeast
- 2 tablespoons olive oil
- Salt and pepper to taste

Directions:

1. Prepare corn grits in accordance with the directions provided on the package, adding shredded sweet potato for the final five minutes of cooking.
2. To soften the onion and garlic, sauté them in olive oil in a skillet until they are tender.
3. To the mixture, add nutritional yeast, Cajun spice, spinach, and salt & pepper to taste. Prepare the spinach until it wilts.
4. Add the spinach combination to the grits made from sweet potatoes.
5. Allow to warm up, and savor the flavors that are laced with Cajun!

23.   VEGAN RED BEANS AND RICE CASSEROLE

Total Time: 1 hour

Prep Time: 20 minutes

Ingredients:

- 2 cups cooked red beans
- 1 cup cooked brown rice
- 1 onion, diced
- 1 bell pepper, diced
- 3 cloves garlic, minced
- 1 can diced tomatoes

- 1 tablespoon Cajun seasoning
- 1 teaspoon thyme
- Salt and pepper to taste
- 2 tablespoons olive oil
- Chopped green onions for garnish

Directions:

1. Set the oven's temperature to 175 degrees Celsius, or 350 degrees F.
2. Sauté the onion, bell pepper, and garlic in olive oil in a skillet until the vegetables have become more tender.
3. Include chopped tomatoes, red beans, rice that has been cooked, Cajun spice, thyme, salt, and pepper in the mixture. Combine thoroughly.
4. In a casserole dish, transfer the mixture and bake it for thirty to forty minutes or until it becomes bubbling.
5. Prior to serving, garnish with green onions that have been chopped.

24.   VEGAN BAYOU BREAKFAST BURRITO

Total Time: 30 minutes

Prep Time: 15 minutes

Ingredients:

- 1 cup tofu scramble (tofu, turmeric, black salt)
- 4 whole-grain tortillas
- 1 cup black beans, cooked

- 1 avocado, sliced
- 1 cup Cajun-spiced hash browns
- 1/2 cup salsa
- Fresh cilantro for garnish

Directions:

1. To prepare the tofu scramble, first crumble the tofu and then fry it with turmeric and black salt.
2. It is possible to reheat the tortillas by using either a microwave or a skillet.
3. It is possible to make burritos by combining tofu scramble, black beans, avocado slices, and hash browns seasoned with Cajun seasoning.
4. Put the burritos in a wrap and add salsa to taste.
5. If you want your burritos to have a crispy texture, you may cook them in the pan.
6. After garnishing your mouthwatering Bayou Breakfast Burrito with fresh cilantro, serve it to your guests.

25.   CORN AND OKRA MAQUE CHOUX

Total Time: 30 minutes

Prep Time: 10 minutes

Ingredients:

- 2 cups fresh or frozen corn kernels
- 1 cup okra, sliced
- 1 bell pepper, diced
- 1 onion, finely chopped
- 3 cloves garlic, minced
- 1 can (14 oz) diced tomatoes
- 1 teaspoon Cajun seasoning
- 1/2 teaspoon smoked paprika
- Salt and pepper to taste
- 2 tablespoons olive oil
- Fresh parsley for garnish

Directions:

1. In a big pan over medium heat, prepare the olive oil.
2. Sauté the onions and garlic until they get a pleasant aroma.
3. Corn, okra, and bell pepper should be added. Within seven to eight minutes, cook the veggies until they are soft.
4. At this stage, you should incorporate diced tomatoes, Cajun spice, smoked paprika, salt, and pepper into the mixture of ingredients.
5. An additional five minutes should be spent simmering.
6. Add some fresh parsley as a garnish, and serve the dish over quinoa or rice.

26.   SPICY TOFU AND COLLARD GREEN TACOS

Total Time: 45 minutes

Prep Time: 15 minutes

Ingredients:

- 1 block extra-firm tofu, pressed and cubed
- 2 cups collard greens, finely chopped
- 1 tablespoon Cajun spice blend
- 1 tablespoon soy sauce
- 1 tablespoon olive oil
- 1 teaspoon hot sauce
- 8 small corn tortillas
- Salsa, avocado, and lime wedges for serving

Directions:

1. The tofu cubes should be tossed in a bowl with the Cajun spice, the soy sauce, and the hot sauce. Delay the marinating process for ten minutes.
2. Get the olive oil heated up to medium-high in a skillet.
3. After adding the tofu that has been marinated, continue to cook it until it is browned on both sides.
4. Prepare the collard greens by adding them to the pan and sautéing them until they wilt.
5. To make the tofu and collard green combination, warm the corn tortillas and then fill them with the ingredients.
6. Accompany the dish with salsa, avocado slices, and wedges of lime.

27. CREOLE CHICKPEA CASSEROLE

Total Time: 1 hour

Prep Time: 20 minutes

Ingredients:

- 2 cans (15 oz each) chickpeas, drained and rinsed
- 1 cup rice, cooked
- 1 onion, diced
- 2 celery stalks, chopped
- 1 bell pepper, diced
- 3 cloves garlic, minced
- 1 can (14 oz) crushed tomatoes
- 1 teaspoon Creole seasoning
- 1/2 teaspoon thyme
- Salt and pepper to taste
- 1 cup vegetable broth
- 2 tablespoons olive oil

Directions:

1. Set the oven's temperature to 375 F. (190 degrees Celsius).
2. Sauté the onions, celery, and bell pepper in olive oil in a large pan until the vegetables have become more tender.
3. Creole spice, garlic, chickpeas, thyme, salt, and pepper should be added to the mixture. Wait an extra five minutes before serving.
4. Place the chickpea mixture in a baking dish and set over the oven. When the rice is done cooking, add smashed tomatoes. Combine thoroughly.
5. Add the vegetable broth to the mixture, then bake it for thirty to thirty-five minutes or until it is bubbling and brown.

28.   VEGAN BOURBON STREET BALLS

Total Time: 1 hour

Prep Time: 15 minutes

Ingredients:

- 2 cups cooked quinoa
- 1 cup black beans, mashed
- 1/2 cup breadcrumbs
- 1/4 cup nutritional yeast
- 2 tablespoons soy sauce

- 2 tablespoons bourbon
- 1 teaspoon smoked paprika
- 1/2 teaspoon garlic powder
- Oil for frying
- Dipping sauce of choice

Directions:

1. Quinoa, mashed black beans, breadcrumbs, nutritional yeast, soy sauce, whiskey, smoked paprika, and garlic powder should be mixed together in a bowl. Blend until well combined.
2. Create balls equal in size to golf balls out of the mixture.
3. In a pan, the oil has to be heated over medium heat. To get a golden brown color on both sides, fry the balls.
4. Take out and place on a paper towel to soak up any excess oil, if there is any.
5. You may serve it with the dipping sauce of your choice.

29.   CAJUN CHICKPEA LETTUCE WRAPS

Total Time: 20 minutes

Prep Time: 10 minutes

Ingredients:

- 1 can (15 oz) chickpeas, drained and rinsed
- 1 tablespoon Cajun seasoning
- 2 tablespoons olive oil
- 1 red bell pepper, diced
- 1 cup cherry tomatoes, halved
- 1/2 cup red onion, finely chopped
- 1 avocado, sliced
- 1 head iceberg lettuce, leaves separated

Directions:

1. Chickpeas should be tossed with Cajun spice in a basin until they are completely covered.
2. Get the olive oil heated up to medium-high in a skillet. After adding the chickpeas, continue cooking them for another five to seven minutes until they become crispy.
3. Put the red onion, cherry tomatoes, and bell pepper into a big bowl and mix them together.
4. Wraps can be created by applying chickpeas, a vegetable combination, and avocado slices to lettuce leaves and then wrapping them.
5. You should serve your Cajun Chickpea Lettuce Wraps right away, and you should enjoy them!

30.   VEGAN BOUDIN QUESADILLAS

Total Time: 30 minutes

Prep Time: 15 minutes

Ingredients:

- 1 cup vegan boudin, crumbled
- 4 large tortillas
- 1 cup vegan cheese, shredded
- 1/2 cup green onions, chopped
- 1/4 cup vegan sour cream

Directions:

1. Crumbled vegan boudin should be cooked in a pan over medium heat until it has a browned appearance.
2. Put one tortilla in a skillet that has been heated, and then add a layer of vegan cheese, boudin that has been cooked, and green onions.
3. After the cheese has melted and the tortilla has turned a golden brown color, place another tortilla on top and continue cooking.
4. Continue doing the same with the remaining tortillas.
5. You may enjoy your Vegan Boudin Quesadillas by slicing them into wedges, serving them with a dollop of vegan sour cream, and eating them!

31.   VEGAN MUFFULETTA WRAPS

Total Time: 15 minutes

Prep Time: 10 minutes

Ingredients:

- 4 large tortillas
- 1 cup vegan olive tapenade
- 1 cup mixed greens
- 1 cup marinated artichoke hearts, chopped
- 1 cup roasted red peppers, sliced
- 1 cup vegan mozzarella, shredded

Directions:

1. Each tortilla should have a substantial amount of vegan olive tapenade spread on it beforehand.
2. For the topping, arrange a mixture of greens, artichoke hearts that have been marinated, roasted red peppers, and vegan mozzarella.
3. Roll each tortilla firmly, and then cut it into pieces that are suitable for snacking.
4. Serve your Vegan Muffuletta Wraps and take the time to taste their delicious flavors!

32. CREOLE STUFFED ACORN SQUASH

Total Time: 1 hour

Prep Time: 15 minutes

Ingredients:

- 2 acorn squashes, halved, and seeds removed
- 1 cup quinoa, cooked
- 1 cup black beans, cooked
- 1 cup corn kernels
- 1 cup diced tomatoes
- 1/2 cup green onions, chopped
- 1 teaspoon Creole seasoning
- 1/2 cup vegan cheese, shredded

Directions:

1. Bring the oven temperature up to 375 °F or 190 °C. Arrange the halves of the acorn squash on a baking sheet with the sliced side down, and bake them for thirty minutes.
2. Combine the quinoa that has been cooked, the black beans, the corn, the tomatoes, the green onions, the Creole spice, and the vegan cheese in a bowl.
3. After removing the squash from the oven, put the quinoa mixture into each side of the squash.
4. To ensure that the squash is soft, continue baking for an additional 15–20 minutes.
5. Indulge in the tastes of Creole Stuffed Acorn Squash when it is still warm and served to you!

33.   CAJUN CORNBREAD

Total Time: 45 minutes

Prep Time: 15 minutes

Ingredients:

- 1 cup cornmeal
- 1 cup all-purpose flour
- 1 tablespoon baking powder
- 1/2 teaspoon baking soda
- 1 teaspoon salt
- 1 cup non-dairy milk (such as almond or soy milk)

- 1/4 cup vegetable oil
- 1/4 cup maple syrup
- 1 cup corn kernels (fresh or frozen)
- 2 tablespoons finely chopped green onions
- 1 teaspoon Cajun seasoning

Directions:

1. Bring the oven temperature up to 375 °F or 190 °C. A square baking pan should be greased.
2. To prepare the batter, in a large basin, mix together the cornmeal, flour, baking powder, baking soda, and salt.
3. Place the non-dairy milk, vegetable oil, and maple syrup in a separate bowl and mix them together.
4. After adding the liquid components to the dry ones, stir the mixture until it is almost completely incorporated.
5. The corn kernels, green onions, and Cajun seasoning should be folded in, as well.
6. Using a toothpick, put in the center, which should come out clean after 25 to 30 minutes in the oven, after which you should pour the mixture into the waiting pan.
7. Hold off on slicing the cornbread until it has cooled down. Serve and take pleasure in it!

34. VEGAN SHRIMP PO'BOY SLIDERS

Total Time: 30 minutes

Prep Time: 15 minutes

Ingredients:

- 1 pound vegan shrimp, peeled and deveined
- 1 cup cornmeal
- 1 teaspoon Cajun seasoning
- 1/2 cup vegan mayonnaise
- 2 tablespoons hot sauce
- 1 tablespoon lemon juice
- 1 cup shredded lettuce
- 1 cup sliced tomatoes
- Slider buns

Directions:

1. Place the vegan shrimp in a bowl and add the cornmeal and Cajun spice. Toss until the shrimp are uniformly covered.
2. The shrimp that have been coated should be cooked in a skillet that is heated over medium heat until they are golden brown, which should take approximately three to four minutes on each side.
3. Vegan mayonnaise, hot sauce, and lemon juice should be mixed in a small bowl to make the spicy mayonnaise. Mix well.
4. Each slider bun should have a large quantity of spicy mayonnaise spread on it.
5. To begin, spread a layer of shredded lettuce on the bottom bun, and then add a few vegan shrimp on top of that.
6. Place sliced tomatoes and the top half of the bun on top of the sandwich.
7. Dish out the vegan shrimp po' boy sliders as soon as possible and appreciate their delectable flavor!

35. VEGAN GRITS AND GREENS

Total Time: 40 minutes

Prep Time: 15 minutes

Ingredients:

- 1 cup grits
- 4 cups vegetable broth
- 1 tablespoon vegan butter
- 1 cup chopped collard greens
- 1 cup chopped kale
- 1 clove garlic, minced
- Salt and pepper to taste
- Hot sauce for serving

Directions:

1. To prepare the vegetable broth, bring it to a boil in a pot. While whisking in the grits, decrease the heat to a low setting.
2. Cook the grits in accordance with the instructions on the package, stirring them constantly.
3. The garlic should be sautéed in vegan butter in a separate skillet until it becomes aromatic.
4. Mix the kale and collard greens together in the pan and cook them until they are wilted and soft.
5. To finish, season the grits with salt and pepper and fold in the greens after they have been cooked.
6. Serve the Vegan Grits and Greens while they are still hot, to taste, with a sprinkle of spicy sauce.

36.   RED PEPPER AND CORNBREAD STUFFING

Total Time: 50 minutes

Prep Time: 20 minutes

Ingredients:

- 8 cups cubed day-old cornbread
- 1/4 cup olive oil
- 1 onion, diced
- 2 celery stalks, diced
- 1 red bell pepper, diced
- 2 cloves garlic, minced
- 1 teaspoon Cajun seasoning
- 1/2 cup vegetable broth
- Salt and pepper to taste
- Fresh parsley for garnish

Directions:

1. Bring the oven temperature up to 375 °F or 190 °C. Prepare a baking dish with butter.
2. In a big pan over medium heat, prepare the olive oil. When the onion, celery, and red bell pepper have become more tender, sauté them.
3. After one minute of frying, add the garlic and Cajun spice to the onion mixture.
4. The cornmeal cubes should be combined with the veggies that have been sautéed in a big pitcher.
5. While mixing the ingredients together, pour the vegetable broth over the mixture. Use pepper and salt to season the food.
6. After transferring the filling to the baking dish that has been prepared, bake it for twenty-five to thirty minutes or until the top is golden brown.
7. Immediately prior to serving, garnish with fresh parsley.

37.   CAJUN-STYLE STUFFED MUSHROOMS

Total Time: 40 minutes

Prep Time: 20 minutes

Servings: 4

Ingredients:

- 16 large mushrooms, cleaned and stems removed
- 1 cup breadcrumbs
- 1/2 cup vegan cream cheese
- 1/4 cup diced red bell pepper
- 1/4 cup diced green onions
- 2 cloves garlic, minced
- 1 teaspoon Cajun seasoning
- Salt and pepper to taste
- Olive oil for drizzling

Directions:

1. Bring the oven temperature up to 375 °F or 190 °C.
2. Combine the breadcrumbs, vegan cream cheese, red bell pepper, green onions, garlic, Cajun spice, salt, and pepper in a bowl. Mix until everything is evenly distributed.
3. A baking sheet should be used to place the mushroom caps once they have been stuffed with the mixture.
4. An olive oil drizzle should be applied to the filled mushrooms.
5. To ensure that the mushrooms are soft and the filling is golden brown, bake the dish for twenty to twenty-five minutes.
6. Cajun-style stuffed mushrooms should be served warm, and they should be enjoyed.

38.　RED PEPPER AND BLACK-EYED PEA SALAD

Total Time: 15 minutes

Prep Time: 15 minutes

Servings: 6

Ingredients:

- 2 cups cooked black-eyed peas
- 1 red bell pepper, diced
- 1/2 cup cherry tomatoes, halved
- 1/4 cup red onion, finely chopped
- 2 tablespoons fresh parsley, chopped
- 2 tablespoons olive oil
- 1 tablespoon apple cider vinegar
- Salt and pepper to taste

Directions:

1. Black-eyed peas, red bell pepper, cherry tomatoes, red onion, and parsley should all be mixed together in a big bowl.
2. An olive oil, apple cider vinegar, salt, and pepper mixture should be mixed together in a small basin using a whisk.
3. After pouring the dressing over the salad, toss it until it is well incorporated.
4. Maintain in the refrigerator for at least half an hour before serving.
5. The Red Pepper and Black-Eyed Pea Salad should be served cold, and you should love it!

39.   SPICY CAJUN CORN CHOWDER

Total Time: 45 minutes

Prep Time: 15 minutes

Servings: 4

Ingredients:

- 2 tablespoons olive oil
- 1 onion, diced
- 2 cloves garlic, minced
- 1 red bell pepper, diced
- 3 cups corn kernels (fresh or frozen)
- 1 teaspoon Cajun seasoning
- 1/2 teaspoon smoked paprika
- 4 cups vegetable broth
- 1 cup potatoes, diced
- 1 cup coconut milk
- Salt and pepper to taste
- Green onions for garnish

Directions:

1. In a big pan over medium heat, prepare the olive oil. Include the red bell pepper, onion, and garlic in the mixture. Sauté the veggies until they have become more tender.
2. Corn, Cajun spice, and smoked paprika should be stirred in at this point. Wait an extra five minutes before serving.
3. Add the potatoes and the veggie stock to the pot. Before lowering the heat and simmering the chowder until the potatoes are thoroughly cooked, bring it to a boil.
4. Add the coconut milk and season it with salt and pepper before stirring it in.
5. For a further ten minutes, continue to simmer.
6. Green onions should be used as a garnish before serving. Enjoy your Corn Chowder with a Spicy Cajun Flavor!

40.   VEGAN ANDOUILLE HASH

Total Time: 30 minutes

Prep Time: 15 minutes

Servings: 4

Ingredients:

- 2 tablespoons vegetable oil
- 1 onion, diced
- 2 bell peppers (any color), diced
- 2 cups diced vegan andouille sausage
- 4 cups cooked potatoes, diced
- 1 teaspoon smoked paprika
- 1/2 teaspoon garlic powder
- Salt and pepper to taste
- Fresh parsley for garnish

Directions:

1. Set the vegetable oil in a big skillet and bring it up to a medium temperature. First, sauté the onion and bell peppers until they have become more tender.
2. Make sure the vegan andouille sausage is browned before adding it to the pan.
3. The diced potatoes, smoked paprika, garlic powder, salt, and pepper should be stirred in at this point. Ensure that the potatoes are cooked until the edges become crunchy.
4. You should serve it warm and garnish it with fresh parsley. Your Vegan Andouille Hash is waiting for you!

41.   CREOLE OKRA AND TOMATOES

Total Time: 30 minutes

Prep Time: 10 minutes

Ingredients:

- 2 cups fresh okra, sliced
- 1 can (14 oz) diced tomatoes, undrained
- 1 onion, finely chopped
- 2 cloves garlic, minced
- 1 bell pepper, diced
- 2 tablespoons olive oil
- 1 teaspoon Cajun seasoning
- Salt and pepper to taste
- Fresh parsley for garnish

Directions:

1. In a big pan over medium heat, prepare the olive oil. To the pan, add the bell pepper, onions, and garlic. Stir-fry the onions until they become transparent.
2. After adding the sliced okra to the skillet, continue to cook it for five minutes while tossing it constantly.
3. The chopped tomatoes, together with their liquid, should be poured in. Cajun seasoning, salt, and pepper need to be added to the dish. Proceed to simmer for a further fifteen minutes.
4. Add some fresh parsley as a garnish, and serve the dish over quinoa or rice.

42.   DIRTY RICE-STUFFED TOMATOES

Total Time: 45 minutes

Prep Time: 20 minutes

Ingredients:

- 4 large tomatoes
- 1 cup brown rice, cooked
- 1 cup black beans, cooked
- 1 onion, finely chopped
- 2 celery stalks, diced
- 1 bell pepper, diced

- 2 cloves garlic, minced
- 1 teaspoon Cajun seasoning
- 1/2 teaspoon paprika
- Salt and pepper to taste
- Chopped green onions for garnish

Directions:

1. Bring the oven up to a temperature of 375 F (190 C).
2. Remove the tops of the tomatoes and remove the pulp from the rest of the tomatoes. Put the tomatoes that have been hollowed out into a baking dish.
3. Combine the rice that has been cooked, the black beans, the onion, the celery, the bell pepper, the garlic, the Cajun spice, the paprika, the salt, and the pepper in a large bowl.
4. Prepare the rice mixture and stuff it inside each tomato.
5. Bake the tomatoes in an oven that has been prepared for twenty-five to thirty minutes or until they are soft.
6. Prior to serving, garnish with green onions that have been chopped.

43.   CAJUN CORN AND POTATO CHOWDER

Total Time: 40 minutes

Prep Time: 15 minutes

Ingredients:

- 2 cups corn kernels (fresh or frozen)
- 2 potatoes, peeled and diced
- 1 onion, finely chopped
- 2 cloves garlic, minced
- 1 bell pepper, diced
- 4 cups vegetable broth
- 1 can (14 oz) coconut milk
- 1 teaspoon Cajun seasoning
- Salt and pepper to taste
- Fresh thyme for garnish

Directions:

1. In a large skillet, sauté the onion, garlic, and bell pepper until they are softened.
2. In a saucepan, combine the following Ingredients: corn, diced potatoes, vegetable broth, and coconut milk. Allow to come to a simmer.
3. Cajun seasoning, salt, and pepper need to be added to the dish. For twenty minutes, or until the potatoes are cooked, simmer the mixture.
4. Fresh thyme should be used as a garnish before serving.

44. VEGAN ZYDECO ZUCCHINI NOODLES

Total Time: 25 minutes

Prep Time: 15 minutes

Ingredients:

- 4 medium zucchini, spiralized into noodles
- 1 cup cherry tomatoes, halved
- 1 cup bell peppers, thinly sliced
- 1/2 cup red onion, thinly sliced
- 2 cloves garlic, minced

- 3 tablespoons olive oil
- 1 teaspoon Cajun seasoning
- Juice of 1 lemon
- Salt and pepper to taste
- Chopped fresh basil for garnish

Directions:

1. In a big pan over medium heat, prepare the olive oil. Sauté the garlic until it achieves a fragrant state.
2. Zucchini noodles, cherry tomatoes, bell peppers, and red onion should be added to the skillet for around five to seven minutes or until the veggies are soft.
3. Cajun seasoning, salt, and pepper need to be added to the dish. Noodles should be tossed with lemon juice after it has been squeezed over them.
4. Prior to serving, garnish with fresh basil that has been chopped.

45. CREOLE-STYLE COLLARD GREEN ROLLS

Total Time: 45 minutes

Prep Time: 20 minutes

Ingredients:

- 1 bunch of collard greens, stems removed
- 1 cup cooked quinoa
- 1 cup black beans, drained and rinsed
- 1 cup diced tomatoes
- 1/2 cup diced red bell pepper
- 1/4 cup diced red onion
- 2 cloves garlic, minced
- 1 teaspoon Cajun seasoning
- Salt and pepper to taste
- 1 tablespoon olive oil
- Lemon wedges for serving

Directions:

1. After two to three minutes in boiling water, collard greens should be blanched. Take out and put to the side.
2. Quinoa, black beans, tomatoes, red bell pepper, red onion, garlic, Cajun spice, salt, and pepper should be combined in a big bowl and then stirred together.
3. A tablespoon of the quinoa mixture should be placed on each collard green leaf, and then the edges should be folded in until the leaf is securely rolled.
4. Get the olive oil heated up to medium-high in a skillet. Cook the collard green rolls for approximately three to four minutes on each side or until they have a small crunch to them.
5. You should serve your Creole-style Collard Green Rolls with lemon wedges, and you should enjoy them!

46.   SWEET POTATO AND BLACK-EYED PEA SALAD

Total Time: 30 minutes

Prep Time: 15 minutes

Ingredients:

- 2 medium sweet potatoes, peeled and diced
- 1 can black-eyed peas, drained and rinsed
- 1 cup cherry tomatoes, halved
- 1/2 cup red onion, finely chopped
- 1/4 cup fresh parsley, chopped
- 2 tablespoons olive oil
- 1 tablespoon apple cider vinegar
- 1 teaspoon Cajun seasoning
- Salt and pepper to taste

Directions:

1. Cook sweet potatoes until they are soft when pierced with a fork so that they can cool down.
2. Sweet potatoes, black-eyed peas, cherry tomatoes, dried red onion, and chopped parsley should be mixed together in a big basin.
3. Olive oil, apple cider vinegar, Cajun spice, salt, and pepper should be mixed together in a small bowl after being whisked together.
4. After pouring the dressing over the salad, carefully mix it to blend the ingredients.
5. Place the Sweet Potato and Black-Eyed Pea Salad in the refrigerator for a few minutes before serving.

47. VEGAN CORNBREAD STUFFING

Total Time: 50 minutes

Prep Time: 15 minutes

Ingredients:

- 6 cups cubed vegan cornbread
- 1 cup celery, finely chopped
- 1 cup onion, finely chopped
- 1 cup mushrooms, sliced
- 2 cloves garlic, minced
- 1 teaspoon dried thyme
- 1 teaspoon dried sage
- 3 cups vegetable broth
- Salt and pepper to taste
- 2 tablespoons olive oil

Directions:

1. Set the oven's temperature to 175 degrees Celsius, or 350 degrees F.
2. Add the garlic, mushrooms, onion, and celery to a large pan and sauté in olive oil until the vegetables are tender.
3. It is suggested to combine the cubed cornmeal, sautéed vegetables, sage, thyme, salt, and pepper in a large dish.
4. After adding the vegetable broth, toss everything together until everything is well combined.
5. After the mixture has been transferred to a baking dish, bake it for thirty to thirty-five minutes or until the top is golden brown.
6. Savor the delectable Vegan Cornbread Stuffing while it is still warm and serve it.

48. CAJUN SWEET POTATO FRIES

Total Time: 40 minutes

Prep Time: 10 minutes

Ingredients:

- 4 medium sweet potatoes, cut into fries
- 2 tablespoons olive oil
- 1 tablespoon Cajun seasoning
- 1 teaspoon paprika
- 1/2 teaspoon garlic powder
- Salt and pepper to taste

Directions:

1. Before you even think of placing the baking pan in the oven, get the temperature up to 425 degrees Fahrenheit (220 degrees Celsius).
2. The sweet potato fries should be tossed in olive oil, Cajun spice, paprika, garlic powder, salt, and pepper in a large bowl. Combine all of the ingredients.
3. The french fries should be arranged in a single layer on the baking pan.
4. Place the fries in the oven and bake for twenty-five to thirty minutes, turning them over halfway through the cooking process.
5. Cajun Sweet Potato Fries are very spicy, so serve them hot and enjoy their deliciousness!

49.   CAJUN EGGPLANT PO' BOY

Total Time: 45 minutes

Prep Time: 15 minutes

Ingredients:

- 1 large eggplant, sliced into 1/2-inch rounds
- 1 cup cornmeal
- 1 cup all-purpose flour
- 1 tablespoon Cajun seasoning
- Salt and pepper to taste
- Vegetable oil for frying
- 4 French rolls
- Vegan mayo
- Shredded lettuce
- Sliced tomatoes
- Pickles

Directions:

1. The cornmeal, flour, Cajun spice, salt, and pepper should be mixed together in a basin.
2. Coat each round of eggplant with the mixture, pressing it firmly to ensure it sticks.
3. Raise the heat to medium-high in a skillet with the oil. Eggplant should be fried until it is golden brown and crispy.
4. On both sides of the buns, smear vegan mayonnaise and slice them.
5. The layers consist of shredded lettuce, pickles, tomatoes, and eggplant that has been fried.
6. As soon as possible, serve and take pleasure in your Cajun Eggplant Po'Boy!

50.   SMOKY CORNBREAD CASSEROLE

Total Time: 1 hour

Prep Time: 15 minutes

Ingredients:

- 2 cups cornmeal
- 1 cup all-purpose flour
- 1 tablespoon baking powder
- 1 teaspoon smoked paprika
- 1 cup corn kernels

- 1 cup unsweetened almond milk
- 1/2 cup olive oil
- 2 tablespoons maple syrup
- 1 teaspoon apple cider vinegar

Directions:

1. Greasing and preheating a baking dish to 375 degrees Fahrenheit (190 degrees Celsius) is the required oven preparation.
2. Gather the cornmeal, flour, baking powder, and smoked paprika into a bowl and mix them together.
3. Put the corn, almond milk, olive oil, maple syrup, and apple cider vinegar into a separate bowl and stir them together.
4. After pouring the liquid components into the dry ones, whisk them together until they are almost completely incorporated.
5. After the baking dish has been prepared, pour the batter into it and bake it for thirty-five to forty minutes or until it reaches a golden brown color.
6. It is recommended that the Smoky Cornbread Casserole be allowed to cool gently before being sliced and served.

51.   VEGAN BANANAS FOSTER PANCAKES

Total Time: 30 minutes

Prep Time: 15 minutes

Ingredients:

- 1 cup all-purpose flour
- 1 tablespoon sugar
- 1 tablespoon baking powder
- 1/2 teaspoon cinnamon
- 1 cup almond milk

- 2 ripe bananas, mashed
- 1 teaspoon vanilla extract
- Vegan butter for cooking
- Maple syrup for serving

Directions:

1. A bowl with a whisk attachment is required for mixing the flour, sugar, baking powder, and cinnamon.
2. Include vanilla essence, mashed bananas, and almond milk in the mixture. Combine until it is completely smooth.
3. Warm up a griddle or a pan that does not stick over medium heat. Apply some vegan butter.
4. Each pancake should have a quarter cup of batter poured onto the griddle. After the bubbles have formed, turn the food and continue cooking until it is golden brown.
5. Maple syrup should be spread on the vegan bananas to foster pancakes before serving.

52. VEGAN GUMBO-STUFFED BELL PEPPER RINGS

Total Time: 1 hour 15 minutes

Prep Time: 30 minutes

Ingredients:

- 4 large bell peppers, halved and seeds removed
- 1 cup okra, sliced
- 1 cup celery, diced
- 1 cup onion, diced
- 1 cup bell pepper, diced
- 3 cloves garlic, minced

- 1 can (14 oz) diced tomatoes
- 1 cup cooked rice
- 4 cups vegetable broth
- 2 tablespoons Cajun seasoning
- Salt and pepper to taste
- Green onions for garnish

Directions:

1. Bring the oven temperature up to 375 °F or 190 °C. Sauté the okra, celery, onion, bell pepper, and garlic in a saucepan until the vegetables have become more tender.
2. Cajun seasoning, Cajun seasoning, chopped tomatoes, cooked rice, vegetable broth, and salt and pepper should be added. Warm for fifteen to twenty minutes.
3. Spread the halves of the bell peppers out in a baking tray. Transfer the gumbo mixture to the pepper halves using a spoon.
4. Peppers should be baked for 25 to 30 minutes or until they are soft.
5. You should serve the Vegan Gumbo-Stuffed Bell Pepper Rings when they are still hot. Garnish them with green onions.

53.   SPICY LENTIL AND OKRA STEW

Total Time: 1 hour

Prep Time: 15 minutes

Ingredients:

- 1 cup dried lentils, rinsed and drained
- 1 lb okra, sliced
- 1 onion, diced
- 3 cloves garlic, minced
- 1 can (14 oz) diced tomatoes
- 4 cups vegetable broth
- 2 tsp Cajun seasoning
- 1 tsp thyme
- Salt and pepper to taste
- 2 tbsp olive oil
- Green onions for garnish

Directions:

1. The chili should simmer for 45 minutes, stirring from time to time, before being turned down to a low simmer.
2. Sauté the onions and garlic until they get a pleasant aroma.
3. Okra, lentils, chopped tomatoes, Cajun spice, thyme, salt, and pepper should be added to the casserole. Give it a good stir.
4. The stew should be brought to a boil once the vegetable broth has been added. Let the lentils boil for forty-five minutes or until they reach the desired tenderness.
5. When necessary, adjust the seasoning. Serve while still hot, with green onions as a garnish.

54. SWEET POTATO BOUDIN BALLS

Total Time: 1 hour 30 minutes

Prep Time: 30 minutes

Ingredients:

- 2 large sweet potatoes, peeled and grated
- 1 cup cooked quinoa
- 1 cup breadcrumbs
- 1/2 cup finely chopped bell pepper
- 1/4 cup finely chopped celery
- 2 tbsp Cajun seasoning
- Salt and pepper to taste
- Oil for frying

Directions:

1. The sweet potatoes, quinoa, breadcrumbs, bell pepper, celery, Cajun spice, salt, and pepper should be mixed together in a big bowl using the food processor. Combine thoroughly.
2. On a baking sheet, shape the mixture into balls and set them in the oven.
3. In a pan, oil has to be heated over medium heat. To get a golden brown color, fry the balls.
4. Once removed, place on paper towels to allow any leftover oil to drain. Serve when still heated.

55. CAJUN ROASTED BRUSSELS SPROUTS

Total Time: 35 minutes

Prep Time: 10 minutes

Ingredients:

- 1 lb Brussels sprouts, trimmed and halved
- 2 tbsp olive oil
- 1 tbsp Cajun seasoning
- 1 tsp garlic powder
- Salt and pepper to taste
- Lemon wedges for serving

Directions:

1. Two hundred degrees Celsius, or 400 degrees Fahrenheit, should be the oven's setting.
2. Olive oil, Cajun spice, garlic powder, salt, and pepper should be mixed together in a basin and then tossed with Brussels sprouts.
3. Position the Brussels sprouts in a single layer on a baking sheet and set it in the oven.
4. For twenty-five to thirty minutes, or until the meat is golden brown and crispy. Place lemon slices on the table.

56.   VEGAN JAMBALAYA-STUFFED ACORN SQUASH

Total Time: 1 hour 15 minutes

Prep Time: 30 minutes

Ingredients:

- 2 acorn squashes, halved, and seeds removed
- 1 cup cooked rice
- 1 can (14 oz) kidney beans, drained
- 1 bell pepper, diced
- 1 onion, diced
- 2 cloves garlic, minced
- 1 cup diced tomatoes
- 2 tsp Cajun seasoning
- 1 tsp thyme
- Salt and pepper to taste
- Chopped parsley for garnish

Directions:

1. Bring the oven temperature up to 375 °F or 190 °C.
2. The cut side of the acorn squash should be facing down when the pieces are arranged on a baking sheet. Bake for 35 to 35 minutes or until the veggies are tender.
3. Sauté the onions, garlic, and bell pepper in a skillet until they have become more tender. Cajun spice, thyme, salt, and pepper should be added, along with tomatoes and kidney beans.
4. Incorporate the cooked rice and bring it to a boil. After the acorn squash halves have been baked, spoon the mixture into them.
5. Before serving, garnish with chopped parsley from the garden.

57. VEGAN BEIGNETS WITH POWDERED SUGAR

Total Time: 2 hours

Prep Time: 1 hour

Ingredients:

- 1 cup all-purpose flour
- 1 tablespoon sugar
- 1 teaspoon baking powder
- 1/4 teaspoon salt
- 1/2 cup plant-based milk
- 1 tablespoon vegetable oil
- 1 teaspoon vanilla extract
- Powdered sugar for dusting

Directions:

1. The flour, sugar, baking powder, and salt should all be combined in a mixing basin before making the batter.
2. Incorporate vanilla essence, vegetable oil, and plant-based milk into the mixture. Until a smooth batter is formed, stir the mixture.
3. Give the batter a half hour to rest before proceeding.
4. A big pot or deep fryer should be heated to 175 degrees Celsius (350 degrees Fahrenheit) for the oil.
5. Spoonfuls of batter should be added to the hot oil and fried until golden brown.
6. The beignets should be removed and drained on paper towels.
7. Sprinkle a good amount of powdered sugar over the top before serving.

58. VEGAN MUFFULETTA WRAP

Total Time: 15 minutes

Prep Time: 15 minutes

Ingredients:

- 1 large tortilla
- 1/2 cup vegan olive tapenade
- 1/4 cup hummus
- 1 cup mixed greens

- 1/2 cup sliced cherry tomatoes
- 1/4 cup sliced red onion
- 1/4 cup sliced black olives
- Salt and pepper to taste

Directions:

1. Olive tapenade and hummus should be distributed equally across the surface of the tortilla once it has been laid down flat.
2. Include cherry tomatoes, red onion, black olives, and mixed greens in the layering process.
3. After seasoning with salt, add pepper and salt to taste.
4. Create a wrap by firmly rolling the tortilla into a ball and fastening it with toothpicks if necessary.
5. Please slice and serve.

59.   CAJUN LENTIL PATTIES

Total Time: 45 minutes

Prep Time: 20 minutes

Ingredients:

- 1 cup cooked lentils
- 1/2 cup breadcrumbs
- 1/4 cup finely chopped onion
- 1/4 cup finely chopped bell pepper
- 2 cloves garlic, minced

- 1 tablespoon Cajun seasoning
- 1 tablespoon flaxseed meal + 3 tablespoons water (flax egg)
- Salt and pepper to taste
- Cooking oil for frying

Directions:

1. In a large basin, mash the lentils that have been cooked.
2. Cajun seasoning, garlic, onion, bell pepper, breadcrumbs, flax egg, salt, and pepper should be added to the mixture, after thoroughly combining, mix.
3. The ingredients should be formed into patties.
4. In a skillet, bring the oil to a setting of medium heat.
5. The patties should be fried until they are golden brown on all sides.
6. After draining on paper towels, serve a meal.

60.   CAJUN-STYLE VEGAN TOFU STIR-FRY

Total Time: 30 minutes

Prep Time: 15 minutes

Ingredients:

- 1 block extra-firm tofu, pressed and cubed
- 2 tablespoons Cajun seasoning
- 2 tablespoons soy sauce
- 1 tablespoon olive oil

- 1 bell pepper, thinly sliced
- 1 red onion, thinly sliced
- 1 cup sliced okra
- 2 cloves garlic, minced
- Cooked rice for serving

Directions:

1. Mix the cubed tofu with the Cajun spice and the soy sauce, making sure that the coating is uniform.
2. Within a large skillet, bring the olive oil to a temperature of medium-high.
3. Cook the tofu until it is browned on all sides after adding it. After removing it from the skillet, set it aside.
4. Once the veggies have reached the desired level of tenderness, sauté the bell pepper, red onion, okra, and garlic in the same pan.
5. After the tofu has finished cooking, return it to the skillet and toss it to blend.
6. While the rice is cooking, serve.

61.   CAJUN TOFU SKEWERS

Total Time: 30 minutes

Prep Time: 15 minutes

Ingredients:

- 1 block of firm tofu, pressed and cubed
- 2 tablespoons Cajun seasoning
- 2 tablespoons olive oil
- 1 bell pepper, cut into chunks
- 1 red onion, cut into wedges
- Wooden skewers soaked in water

Directions:

1. The diced tofu, Cajun spice, and olive oil should be mixed together in a basin or bowl. Ensure that it is marinated for a minimum of ten minutes.
2. When ready to use, preheat a grill or grill pan over medium-high heat.
3. Skewer the tofu, bell pepper, and red onion that have been marinated on the wooden skewers that have been soaked.
4. For approximately five to seven minutes on each side, grill the skewers or until the tofu is golden brown and the veggies are soft.
5. Be sure to serve these tasty Cajun tofu Skewers when they are still hot.

62.   SPICY CAJUN ZUCCHINI NOODLES

Total Time: 20 minutes

Prep Time: 10 minutes

Ingredients:

- 4 medium-sized zucchinis, spiralized
- 2 tablespoons olive oil
- 3 cloves garlic, minced
- 1 teaspoon Cajun seasoning
- 1/2 teaspoon red pepper flakes (adjust to taste)
- Salt and black pepper, to taste
- Fresh parsley, chopped (for garnish)

Directions:

1. In a big saucepan, boil the olive oil until it simmers over medium heat. After adding the garlic, sauté it until it becomes aromatic.
2. Cajun spice, red pepper flakes, salt, and black pepper should be added to the zucchini noodles; then, the noodles should be tossed in the skillet.
3. Continue to sauté the zucchini noodles for five to seven minutes or until they are cooked but still have a small crunch.
4. A pleasant and spicy Cajun Zucchini Noodles experience may be had by garnishing the dish with fresh parsley and serving it immediately.

63.   VEGAN ZYDECO MUSHROOM SKEWERS

Total Time: 35 minutes

Prep Time: 20 minutes

Ingredients:

- 16 oz mushrooms, cleaned and halved
- 1/4 cup soy sauce
- 2 tablespoons Cajun seasoning
- 2 tablespoons olive oil
- 1 tablespoon maple syrup
- Wooden skewers soaked in water

Directions:

1. To create the marinade, put the soy sauce, maple syrup, olive oil, and Cajun spice in a bowl and stir to incorporate.
2. After adding the mushrooms to the marinade, make sure that they are well covered. At the very least, give them fifteen minutes to marinade.
3. The grill or pan should be heated to a medium-high temperature before you begin.
4. Place mushrooms that have been marinated on wooden skewers that have been soaked, and cook them for eight to ten minutes, flipping them regularly.
5. Serve these vegan Zydeco mushroom skewers with your preferred dipping sauce on the side.

64.   CAJUN-STYLE VEGAN CHILI

Total Time: 1 hour

Prep Time: 15 minutes

Ingredients:

- 2 tablespoons olive oil
- 1 onion, diced
- 3 cloves garlic, minced
- 1 bell pepper, diced
- 2 celery stalks, diced
- 1 can (15 oz) kidney beans, drained and rinsed
- 1 can (15 oz) black beans, drained and rinsed

- 1 can (28 oz) crushed tomatoes
- 1 cup corn kernels
- 2 tablespoons tomato paste
- 3 tablespoons Cajun seasoning
- Salt and black pepper, to taste
- Optional toppings: sliced green onions, vegan cheese, cilantro

Directions:

1. Reach a medium temperature for the olive oil in a large pot. Include celery, onion, garlic, and bell pepper in the mixture. For vegetables to become more tender, sauté them.
2. The following ingredients should be added: kidney beans, black beans, crushed tomatoes, corn, tomato paste, Cajun seasoning, crushed black pepper, and salt. To combine, give it a thorough stir.
3. The chili should simmer for 45 minutes, stirring from time to time, before being turned down to a low simmer.
4. When necessary, adjust the seasoning. Cajun-style vegan chili should be served hot, with sliced green onions, vegan cheese, or cilantro on top, depending on your preference.

65. VEGAN BLACKENED MUSHROOM TACOS

Total Time: 30 minutes

Prep Time: 15 minutes

Servings: 4

Ingredients:

- 1 pound fresh mushrooms, cleaned and sliced
- 2 tablespoons Cajun seasoning
- 2 tablespoons olive oil
- 1 red onion, thinly sliced
- 1 bell pepper, thinly sliced
- 1 cup shredded lettuce
- 1 cup diced tomatoes
- 1/2 cup chopped fresh cilantro
- 8 small corn tortillas
- Lime wedges for serving

Directions:

1. Cajun seasoning should be tossed with sliced mushrooms in a large bowl until the mushrooms are completely covered.
2. A saucepan filled with olive oil should be heated to a simmer over medium-high heat. Add the seasoned mushrooms and cook until blackened and tender, about 5-7 minutes.
3. The tortillas should be warmed for approximately thirty seconds on each side in a separate skillet.
4. Before you assemble the tacos, top each tortilla with a dollop of the charred mushrooms. Top with sliced onions, bell peppers, lettuce, tomatoes, and cilantro.
5. Accompany the tacos with slices of lime.
6. Enjoy your Vegan Blackened Mushroom Tacos!

66. CAJUN CHICKPEA AND ARTICHOKE SALAD

Total Time: 20 minutes

Prep Time: 10 minutes

Servings: 6

Ingredients:

- 2 cans (15 oz each) chickpeas, drained and rinsed
- 1 can (14 oz) artichoke hearts, drained and chopped
- 1 cup cherry tomatoes, halved
- 1/2 red onion, finely chopped
- 1/4 cup chopped fresh parsley
- 2 tablespoons Cajun seasoning
- 3 tablespoons olive oil
- 2 tablespoons red wine vinegar
- Salt and pepper to taste

Directions:

1. Chickpeas, artichoke hearts that have been diced, cherry tomatoes, red onion, and parsley should be mixed together in a big bowl.
2. A small bowl should be used to combine Cajun spice, olive oil, and red wine vinegar by whisking them together.
3. After pouring the dressing over the salad, toss it until it is well incorporated. After seasoning with salt, add pepper and salt to taste.
4. Prior to serving, allow the dish to chill in the refrigerator for a minimum of ten minutes. This Cajun Chickpea and Artichoke Salad is a delightful side dish that you may serve to your guests.

67.   VEGAN MAQUE CHOUX FLATBREAD

Total Time: 45 minutes

Prep Time: 20 minutes

Servings: 4

Ingredients:

- 1 batch of your favorite pizza dough
- 1 tablespoon olive oil
- 1 red bell pepper, diced
- 1 green bell pepper, diced
- 1 cup fresh or frozen corn kernels
- 1 cup diced tomatoes
- 1 cup sliced okra
- 2 cloves garlic, minced
- 2 teaspoons Cajun seasoning
- Salt and pepper to taste
- 1 cup vegan mozzarella cheese, shredded
- Fresh parsley for garnish

Directions:

1. In accordance with the directions provided for the pizza dough, preheat your oven.
2. On a surface that has been dusted with flour, roll out the pizza dough and then move it to a baking sheet.
3. Get the olive oil ready by warming it in a skillet over medium heat. Cajun seasoning, chopped bell peppers, corn, tomatoes, sliced okra, garlic, and salt and pepper are the ingredients that should be included. This should take around seven to ten minutes or until the veggies are soft.
4. Spread the vegetable mixture that has been sautéed in a uniform layer over the pizza dough. The vegan mozzarella cheese should be sprinkled on top.
5. If the pizza dough package doesn't specify how long to bake the dough, then follow those directions. Brown the crust and melt the cheese in the oven until the pizza is bubbly and golden.
6. Incorporate fresh parsley and slice it as a garnish. Eat your Vegan Maque Choux Flatbread with pleasure!

68.   OKRA AND TOMATO GUMBO

Total Time: 1 hour

Prep Time: 20 minutes

Servings: 6

Ingredients:

- 2 tablespoons vegetable oil
- 1 cup okra, sliced
- 1 onion, diced
- 1 bell pepper, diced
- 2 celery stalks, diced
- 3 cloves garlic, minced
- 1 can (14 oz) diced tomatoes

- 4 cups vegetable broth
- 1 cup sliced mushrooms
- 1 cup cooked chickpeas
- 2 teaspoons Cajun seasoning
- 1 teaspoon dried thyme
- Salt and pepper to taste
- Cooked rice for serving

Directions:

1. In a large saucepan, bring the vegetable oil to a temperature of medium. Include garlic, okra, onion, bell pepper, and celery in the mixture. Sauté the veggies for around eight to ten minutes or until they have become more tender.
2. Cajun seasoning, thyme, salt, and pepper should be added to the mixture, along with chopped tomatoes, vegetable broth, mushrooms, and chickpeas. Turn the heat down to low and simmer for 30–40 minutes after it boils.
3. Okra and tomato gumbo should be served over rice that has been cooked. Should you so want, garnish with some fresh parsley. Have a delicious gumbo that is influenced by Cajun cuisine!

69.   SPICY QUINOA AND OKRA SKILLET

Total Time: 30 minutes

Prep Time: 10 minutes

Ingredients:

- 1 cup quinoa, rinsed
- 2 cups water
- 1 tablespoon olive oil
- 1 onion, diced
- 2 cloves garlic, minced
- 1 bell pepper, diced

- 1 cup okra, sliced
- 1 can (14 oz) diced tomatoes
- 1 teaspoon Cajun seasoning
- Salt and pepper to taste
- Fresh parsley for garnish

Directions:

1. Bring the quinoa and water together in a medium-sized pot. After bringing it to a boil, decrease the heat to low, cover it, and continue to simmer for fifteen minutes or until the quinoa is cooked and the water has been absorbed.
2. Get the olive oil ready by warming it in a skillet over medium heat. Onion and garlic should be added and sautéed until aromatic.
3. After the vegetables are done cooking, throw in the okra and bell pepper and keep cooking.
4. After the quinoa has been cooked, add chopped tomatoes, Cajun spice, salt, and pepper to the mixture. Wait an extra five minutes before serving.
5. Immediately prior to serving, garnish with fresh parsley. Have fun eating your skillet of spicy quinoa and okra soup!

70.   CAJUN STUFFED PEPPERS

Total Time: 45 minutes

Prep Time: 20 minutes

Ingredients:

- 4 large bell peppers, halved and seeds removed
- 1 cup cooked brown rice
- 1 can (15 oz) black beans, drained and rinsed
- 1 cup corn kernels
- 1 cup diced tomatoes
- 1 onion, finely chopped
- 2 cloves garlic, minced
- 2 teaspoons Cajun seasoning
- Salt and pepper to taste
- 1 cup vegan cheese, shredded (optional)
- Fresh cilantro for garnish

Directions:

1. Bring the oven temperature up to 375 °F or 190 °C. Brown rice that has been cooked, black beans, corn, tomatoes, onion, garlic, Cajun spice, salt, and pepper should be mixed together in a wide and spacious dish.
2. When you have finished stuffing each half of the bell pepper with the mixture, place them on a baking dish.
3. If you so want, vegan cheese can be sprinkled on top of each pepper that has been packed.
4. The casserole should be covered with foil and baked for twenty-five to thirty minutes or until the peppers are soft.
5. Fresh cilantro should be used as a garnish before serving. Your peppers stuffed with Cajun seasoning are now ready to be eaten!

71.   CAJUN BLACK BEAN JAMBALAYA

Total Time: 40 minutes

Prep Time: 15 minutes

Ingredients:

- 1 cup long-grain brown rice
- 2 cups vegetable broth
- 1 tablespoon olive oil
- 1 onion, diced
- 1 bell pepper, diced
- 2 celery stalks, chopped
- 3 cloves garlic, minced

- 1 can (15 oz) black beans, drained and rinsed
- 1 can (14 oz) diced tomatoes
- 2 teaspoons Cajun seasoning
- 1 teaspoon thyme
- Salt and pepper to taste
- Green onions for garnish

Directions:

1. The rice and the vegetable broth should be combined in a saucepan. Rice should be prepared by bringing it to a boil, then lowering the heat to a low setting, covering the pot, and simmering it for twenty minutes.
2. Get the olive oil ready by warming it in a skillet over medium heat. Include garlic, onion, bell pepper, and celery in the mixture. To ensure that the veggies are cooked through.
3. Black beans, chopped tomatoes, Cajun spice, thyme, salt, and pepper should be well combined and stirred in. Wait an extra ten minutes before serving.
4. After the rice has been cooked, add it to the black bean mixture in the skillet and thoroughly combine the two.
5. Prior to serving, garnish with green onions that have been chopped. Have fun eating your Jambalaya with Cajun Black Beans!

72. VEGAN JAMBALAYA CASSEROLE

Total Time: 1 hour

Prep Time: 25 minutes

Ingredients:

- 1 cup brown rice
- 2 1/2 cups vegetable broth
- 1 tablespoon olive oil
- 1 onion, diced
- 1 bell pepper, diced
- 2 celery stalks, chopped
- 3 cloves garlic, minced

- 1 can (15 oz) kidney beans, drained and rinsed
- 1 can (14 oz) diced tomatoes
- 1 cup sliced okra
- 2 teaspoons Cajun seasoning
- 1 teaspoon smoked paprika
- Salt and pepper to taste
- Fresh parsley for garnish

Directions:

1. Bring the oven temperature up to 375 °F or 190 °C.To make the brown rice, blend it with the vegetable broth in a pot. First, bring it to a boil, then immediately decrease the heat to low, cover it, and continue to simmer for thirty minutes or until the rice is done.
2. Get the olive oil ready by warming it in a skillet over medium heat. Include garlic, onion, bell pepper, and celery in the mixture. To ensure that the veggies are cooked through.
3. The kidney beans, diced tomatoes, sliced okra, Cajun spice, smoked paprika, salt, and pepper should be stirred in at this point. Wait an extra ten minutes before serving.
4. A casserole dish should be used to combine the rice that has been cooked with the veggie combination. After thoroughly combining the ingredients, bake them for fifteen to twenty minutes or until they are completely warm.
5. Immediately prior to serving, garnish with fresh parsley. Jambalaya casserole made with vegan ingredients is now ready to be served.

73.   VEGAN MUFFULETTA PINWHEELS

Total Time: 30 minutes

Prep Time: 15 minutes

Ingredients:

- 1 package of vegan puff pastry sheets
- 1 cup mixed olives, chopped
- 1/2 cup roasted red peppers, diced
- 1/2 cup marinated artichoke hearts, chopped
- 1/2 cup vegan mozzarella cheese, shredded
- 1/4 cup vegan pesto
- 1 tablespoon Cajun seasoning
- Fresh parsley for garnish

Directions:

1. Bring the oven temperature up to 375 °F or 190 °C. Place the sheets of puff pastry on a surface that has been lightly dusted with flour.
2. Olives, roasted red peppers, artichoke hearts, vegan mozzarella, pesto, and Cajun spice should be combined in a bowl and then mixed together again.
3. The ingredients should be spread out evenly on the pieces of puff pastry.
4. Assemble the pastry sheets into a log by rolling them up tightly.
5. Pinwheels should be made from the logs, and then they should be placed on a baking pan.
6. For fifteen to twenty minutes, or until the top is golden brown.
7. Immediately prior to serving, garnish with fresh parsley.

74.   CAJUN CAULIFLOWER AND BLACK BEAN BURRITOS

Total Time: 40 minutes

Prep Time: 20 minutes

Ingredients:

- 2 cups cauliflower florets, roasted
- 1 can black beans, drained and rinsed
- 1 cup cooked quinoa
- 1 cup diced tomatoes
- 1/2 cup red onion, finely chopped
- 1/4 cup fresh cilantro, chopped
- 2 tablespoons Cajun seasoning
- 4 large whole wheat tortillas
- Avocado slices for serving

Directions:

1. Cook the cauliflower in the oven at 400 degrees Fahrenheit (200 degrees Celsius) until it is soft.
2. Cajun seasoning, roasted cauliflower, black beans, quinoa, tomatoes, red onion, cilantro, and additional ingredients should be mixed together in a big bowl.
3. Place a spoonful of the mixture on each tortilla once it has been warmed somewhat.
4. Prepare burritos by rolling the tortillas into a ball and placing them on a baking tray with the seam side down.
5. Burritos should be baked for ten to fifteen minutes or until they are completely hot.
6. Add slices of avocado to the top of the dish.

75. VEGAN GRITS WITH SMOKY TOMATO SAUCE

Total Time: 45 minutes

Prep Time: 15 minutes

Ingredients:

- 1 cup grits
- 4 cups vegetable broth
- 1 can diced tomatoes
- 1 onion, finely chopped
- 3 cloves garlic, minced

- 1 teaspoon smoked paprika
- 1/2 teaspoon cayenne pepper
- Salt and pepper to taste
- Chopped green onions for garnish

Directions:

1. To prepare the vegetable broth, bring it to a boil in a pot. While whisking the grits in slowly, decrease the heat to a low setting. Cook until the mixture has thickened, stirring now and again.
2. In a different pan, sauté the garlic and onions until they soften.
3. Salt, pepper, chopped tomatoes, smoked paprika, and cayenne pepper should be added to the mixture. Warm for fifteen to twenty minutes.
4. The creamy grits should be served with the smokey tomato sauce on top.
5. Chopped green onions should be used as a garnish.

76.   DIRTY RICE AND LENTIL LETTUCE WRAPS

Total Time: 50 minutes

Prep Time: 20 minutes

Ingredients:

- 1 cup brown lentils, cooked
- 1 cup brown rice, cooked
- 1 onion, diced
- 1 bell pepper, diced
- 3 cloves garlic, minced
- 1 cup celery, chopped

- 1 cup vegetable broth
- 2 tablespoons Cajun seasoning
- 1 teaspoon thyme
- 1 teaspoon hot sauce (optional)
- Lettuce leaves for wrapping

Directions:

1. To soften the onions, bell pepper, and garlic, sauté them in a large pan until they are tender.
2. The lentils, rice, celery, vegetable broth, Cajun spice, thyme, and spicy sauce should be added after they have been cooked. Give it a good stir.
3. For twenty to twenty-five minutes, simmer until the flavors combine.
4. For the purpose of making wraps, spoon the dirty rice and lentil mixture onto the leaves of the lettuce.
5. Serve as soon as possible.

77.   CAJUN RED BEANS AND RICE

Total Time: 1 hour 30 minutes

Prep Time: 15 minutes

Servings: 4

Ingredients:

- 1 cup dried red beans, soaked overnight
- 1 onion, finely chopped
- 2 celery stalks, diced
- 1 green bell pepper, chopped
- 3 cloves garlic, minced
- 1 teaspoon thyme

- 1 teaspoon oregano
- 1 teaspoon smoked paprika
- 1 bay leaf
- Salt and pepper to taste
- 2 cups cooked brown rice
- Green onions, sliced (for garnish)

Directions:

1. The red beans that have been soaked should be combined with diced onion, celery, bell pepper, and garlic in a big saucepan.
2. Garnish with smoked paprika, bay leaf, thyme, oregano, and season with salt and pepper. Covering the mixture with water will bring it to a boil.
3. Cover and lower heat to low after bringing to a boil. Boil for one hour or until the beans are cooked.
4. Over the brown rice that has been cooked, serve the red beans. To finish, garnish with sliced green onions.

78.   CAJUN COLLARD GREENS WITH SMOKED TOFU

Total Time: 45 minutes

Prep Time: 15 minutes

Servings: 4

Ingredients:

- 1 bunch collard greens, stems removed and leaves chopped
- 1 tablespoon olive oil
- 1 onion, finely chopped
- 2 cloves garlic, minced
- 1 cup smoked tofu, diced
- 1 teaspoon Cajun seasoning
- Salt and pepper to taste
- Hot sauce (optional)

Directions:

1. Simmer the olive oil in a large pan over medium heat.
2. Sauté the chopped onion and garlic until they have become more pliable.
3. Cook the smoked tofu in chopped form until it reaches a golden brown color.
4. Collard greens, Cajun spice, salt, and pepper should be added to the dish. Greens should be cooked until they are wilted and soft.
5. Serve while still hot, and if desired, sprinkle with spicy sauce.

79.   VEGAN GUMBO-STUFFED ACORN SQUASH

Total Time: 1 hour 15 minutes

Prep Time: 30 minutes

Servings: 4

Ingredients:

- 2 acorn squashes, halved, and seeds removed
- 1 cup okra, sliced
- 1 cup bell peppers, diced
- 1 cup celery, chopped
- 1 onion, finely chopped
- 3 cloves garlic, minced
- 1 can diced tomatoes
- 4 cups vegetable broth
- 1 teaspoon thyme
- 1 teaspoon gumbo file powder
- Salt and pepper to taste
- Cooked white rice (for serving)

Directions:

1. Bring the oven temperature up to 375 °F or 190 °C.
2. Spread out the acorn squash halves on a baking sheet and cut the sides down. Bake for forty to forty-five minutes or until the vegetables are soft.
3. Sauté the onion, garlic, okra, bell peppers, and celery in a large saucepan until the vegetables have become more tender.
4. Diced tomatoes, vegetable broth, thyme, gumbo file powder, salt, and pepper should be added to the ingredients. Simmer for twenty to twenty-five minutes.
5. After the acorn squash halves have been baked, spoon the gumbo mixture into them on top of the white rice that has been cooked.

80.   QUINOA AND CORNBREAD MUFFINS

Total Time: 35 minutes

Prep Time: 15 minutes

Servings: 12

Ingredients:

- 1 cup quinoa, rinsed and cooked
- 1 cup cornmeal
- 1 cup all-purpose flour
- 1 tablespoon baking powder
- 1/2 teaspoon salt
- 1 cup almond milk
- 1/4 cup maple syrup
- 1/4 cup coconut oil, melted
- 1 flax egg (1 tablespoon ground flaxseed + 3 tablespoons water)
- 1 cup corn kernels (fresh or frozen)

Directions:

1. Bring the oven temperature up to 375 °F or 190 °C.
2. Use paper liners or a muffin tray that has been greased.
3. Cornmeal, flour, baking powder, and salt should be mixed together in a separate, big basin.
4. The flax egg, maple syrup, melted coconut oil, and almond milk should be combined in a separate bowl and mixed carefully.
5. To the dry ingredients, add the wet components and whisk until the ingredients are just incorporated. The cooked quinoa and corn kernels should be folded in.
6. The muffins should be baked for 18–20 minutes or until a toothpick inserted in the middle of each muffin comes out clean after each muffin pan has been filled.
7. After the muffins have cooled, they may be served.

81.   MARDI GRAS VEGGIE SKEWERS

Total Time: 30 minutes

Prep Time: 15 minutes

Serving: 4

Ingredients:

- 1 medium zucchini, sliced
- 1 red bell pepper, cut into chunks
- 1 yellow bell pepper, cut into chunks
- 1 red onion, cut into wedges
- 8 cherry tomatoes
- 1/4 cup olive oil
- 2 tablespoons Cajun seasoning
- 1 tablespoon lemon juice
- Salt and pepper to taste
- Wooden skewers soaked in water

Directions:

1. First, bring the grill or grill pan up to a temperature of medium-high.
2. Cajun spice, lemon juice, salt, and pepper should be mixed together in a dish with olive oil. To create a mixture, stir.
3. The veggies should be threaded onto the skewers in a manner that alternates between the various vegetables.
4. Use the Cajun spice mixture to coat the skewers in a light coating.
5. To ensure that the veggies are soft and have a small charred appearance, grill the skewers for eight to ten minutes, flipping them regularly.
6. Enjoy the vivid taste of Mardi Gras on a stick as soon as possible by serving it immediately.

82.   CREOLE-STYLE CHICKPEA STEW

Total Time: 45 minutes

Prep Time: 15 minutes

Cook Time: 30 minutes

Serving: 6

Ingredients:

- 2 cans (15 oz each) chickpeas, drained and rinsed
- 1 onion, finely chopped
- 2 bell peppers (any color), diced
- 3 celery stalks, chopped
- 3 cloves garlic, minced
- 1 can (14 oz) diced tomatoes
- 2 cups vegetable broth
- 2 tablespoons tomato paste
- 1 tablespoon Cajun seasoning
- 1 teaspoon dried thyme
- Salt and pepper to taste
- 2 tablespoons olive oil
- Cooked rice for serving

Directions:

1. To prepare the olive oil, place it in a big pot and bring it to a simmer without letting it boil. Include celery, onions, and bell peppers in the dish. To ensure that the veggies are cooked through.
2. Garlic should be added and cooked for an additional one to two minutes.
3. The chickpeas, chopped tomatoes, tomato paste, Cajun spice, thyme, salt, and pepper should be stirred in at this point.
4. Once the vegetable broth has been added, bring the mixture to a simmer. Cover and allow it to simmer for twenty-five to thirty minutes, tossing it halfway through.
5. Serve this substantial chickpea stew over rice that has been prepared, and taste the abundant Creole flavors that it possesses.

83.   VEGAN RED PEPPER GRITS

Total Time: 40 minutes

Prep Time: 10 minutes

Cook Time: 30 minutes

Serving: 4

Ingredients:

- 1 cup grits
- 4 cups vegetable broth
- 1 cup almond milk
- 2 red bell peppers, roasted and chopped
- 1/2 cup nutritional yeast
- 2 tablespoons vegan butter
- Salt and pepper to taste

Directions:

1. Both the vegetable broth and the almond milk should be brought to a boil in a pot.
2. While stirring continually, gradually incorporate the grits into the mixture using a whisk.
3. Take the pot off the heat, cover it, and let it simmer for twenty to twenty-five minutes or until the grits are creamy and soft.
4. Roasted red peppers, nutritional yeast, vegan butter, freshly ground black pepper, and salt should be stirred in.
5. Continue to cook for a further five minutes, stirring the mixture each time.
6. If you serve the vegan red pepper grits hot, you will be able to appreciate their velvety consistency and robust taste.

84.   SPICY OKRA AND CORN GRITS CAKES

Total Time: 50 minutes

Prep Time: 20 minutes

Cook Time: 30 minutes

Serving: 8

Ingredients:

- 1 cup corn grits
- 3 cups water
- 1 cup okra, chopped
- 1 cup corn kernels
- 1/2 cup green onions, chopped
- 1 jalapeño, seeded and finely chopped
- 1/4 cup fresh parsley, chopped
- 1/4 cup flaxseed meal mixed with 1/2 cup water (as an egg substitute)
- 1 teaspoon Cajun seasoning
- Salt and pepper to taste
- Cooking oil for frying

Directions:

1. Boiling water requires the use of a pot. Whip in the corn grits gently while reducing the heat to low, covering the pot, and simmering for twenty minutes.
2. Grits that have been cooked, okra that has been diced, corn kernels, green onions, jalapeño, parsley, flaxseed meal mixture, Cajun spice, salt, and pepper should be mixed together in a big bowl.
3. To make the mixture more solid, shape it into patties and place them in the refrigerator for ten to fifteen minutes.
4. Raise the heat to medium-high in a skillet with the oil. Cook the grits cakes in a skillet until they get a golden brown color.
5. While still heated, drain on paper towels and serve. The addition of these spicy grits cakes to your Cajun vegan cuisine is sure to provide a wonderful experience.

85.   SPICY CAJUN TEMPEH STIR-FRY

Total Time: 30 minutes

Prep Time: 15 minutes

Ingredients:

- 1 package (8 oz) tempeh, cubed
- 2 tablespoons Cajun seasoning
- 2 tablespoons soy sauce
- 1 tablespoon olive oil
- 1 bell pepper, thinly sliced
- 1 red onion, thinly sliced
- 1 cup broccoli florets
- 3 cloves garlic, minced
- 2 tablespoons tomato paste
- 2 tablespoons water
- Cooked rice for serving
- Fresh cilantro for garnish

Directions:

1. The tempeh cubes should be tossed in a bowl with the Cajun spice and the soy sauce. Marinate it for ten minutes before serving.
2. A big pan should be heated to a simmer with the olive oil over medium heat. sauté the tempeh that has been marinated until it is golden brown.
3. Incorporate garlic, broccoli, red onion, and bell pepper into the dish. Vegetables should be cooked until they are crisp-tender.
4. Combine tomato paste and water in a small dish and stir well. Over the stir-fry, pour the sauce, and then whisk to blend.
5. On top of the rice that has been cooked, serve the spicy Cajun tempeh stir-fry. Serve with a garnish of fresh cilantro.

86.   VEGAN MAQUE CHOUX TACOS

Total Time: 40 minutes

Prep Time: 20 minutes

Ingredients:

- 1 cup corn kernels
- 1 red bell pepper, diced
- 1 green bell pepper, diced
- 1 small zucchini, diced
- 1 small red onion, finely chopped
- 2 cloves garlic, minced

- 1 tablespoon Cajun seasoning
- 1 cup cherry tomatoes, halved
- 1 avocado, sliced
- 8 small corn tortillas
- Fresh cilantro for garnish
- Lime wedges for serving

Directions:

1. Once the veggies have reached the desired level of tenderness, sauté the corn, red and green bell peppers, zucchini, red onion, and garlic in a pan.
2. Once the veggies have been coated with Cajun seasoning, give them a thorough toss.
3. Continue to simmer for an additional three minutes after adding the cherry tomatoes.
4. To make the Maque Choux combination, warm corn tortillas and fill each one with the ingredients.
5. Spread slices of avocado on top, then garnish with chopped fresh cilantro. Lime wedges should be served on the side.

87. CAJUN CORN AND AVOCADO TOAST

Total Time: 15 minutes

Prep Time: 10 minutes

Ingredients:

- 4 slices whole-grain bread
- 1 cup corn kernels (fresh or frozen)
- 1 tablespoon Cajun seasoning
- 1 avocado, mashed

- 2 tablespoons lime juice
- Salt and pepper to taste
- Red pepper flakes for garnish (optional)
- Chopped fresh parsley for garnish

Directions:

1. Depending on your preferences, toast the bread pieces.
2. Cajun seasoning should be used to sauté corn in a pan until it is completely heated through.
3. A bowl should be used to combine the mashed avocado, lime juice, salt, and pepper, and then stir the mixture together.
4. After the bread pieces have been toasted, spread the avocado mixture on top of them equally.
5. Cajun corn should be placed on top, and chopped parsley and crushed red pepper should be used as garnishes.

88. SPICY CAJUN TOFU TACOS

Total Time: 35 minutes

Prep Time: 20 minutes

Ingredients:

- 1 block firm tofu, pressed and crumbled
- 2 tablespoons Cajun seasoning
- 2 tablespoons olive oil
- 1 red bell pepper, sliced
- 1 yellow bell pepper, sliced
- 1 small red onion, thinly sliced
- 1 cup shredded lettuce
- 8 small corn tortillas
- Vegan sour cream for serving
- Fresh cilantro for garnish

Directions:

1. Cajun seasoning should be tossed with crushed tofu until it is well covered.
2. Get the olive oil heated up to medium-high in a skillet. To make the seasoned tofu crispy, sauté it after you've added it.
3. Toss in the bell peppers and chopped red onion, then mix everything together. Let the vegetables simmer until they reach a soft texture.
4. To make the spicy Cajun tofu combination, warm corn tortillas and fill them with the ingredients.
5. As a finishing touch, top with shredded lettuce, vegan sour cream, and fresh cilantro.

89.   SWEET POTATO AND LENTIL GUMBO

Total Time: 1 hour 30 minutes

Prep Time: 20 minutes

Ingredients:

- 1 cup dried green or brown lentils, rinsed
- 2 large sweet potatoes, peeled and diced
- 1 onion, finely chopped
- 3 celery stalks, chopped
- 1 bell pepper, diced
- 3 cloves garlic, minced
- 1 can (28 oz) crushed tomatoes
- 4 cups vegetable broth
- 1 tablespoon Cajun seasoning
- 1 teaspoon thyme
- 1 teaspoon smoked paprika
- Salt and pepper to taste
- 2 tablespoons olive oil
- Green onions, chopped (for garnish)
- Cooked rice (for serving)

Directions:

1. Transfer the olive oil to a medium-high heat in a big saucepan. The garlic, onions, celery, and bell pepper should be added. To ensure that the veggies are cooked through.
2. Combine the sweet potatoes, lentils, crushed tomatoes, vegetable broth, Cajun spice, thyme, smoked paprika, salt, and pepper. Stir until everything is evenly distributed.
3. Increase the heat to a boil and cook the lentils for about 1 hour or until they are the desired softness. When necessary, adjust the seasoning. A garnish of chopped green onions should be placed on top of the cooked rice dish.

90.   VEGAN ANDOUILLE STUFFED MUSHROOMS

Total Time: 40 minutes

Prep Time: 15 minutes

Ingredients:

- 1 pound large mushrooms, stems removed and reserved
- 1 cup cooked quinoa
- 1/2 cup vegan andouille sausage, finely chopped
- 1/4 cup onion, finely chopped
- 2 cloves garlic, minced

- 1 teaspoon Cajun seasoning
- 1/2 cup breadcrumbs
- 2 tablespoons olive oil
- Salt and pepper to taste
- Fresh parsley, chopped (for garnish)

Directions:

1. Before you start baking, get your oven up to 375 F (190 C).
2. The mushroom stems that have been retained should be chopped and then sautéed with onion, garlic, and vegan andouille sausage until they are cooked.
3. Place the cooked quinoa, the combination that has been sautéed, the Cajun spice, the breadcrumbs, the salt, and the pepper in a bowl.
4. After you've stuffed all of the mushroom caps with the mixture, set them on a baking sheet.
5. The stuffed mushrooms should be baked for twenty-five to thirty minutes or until the mushrooms have reached the desired level of tenderness.
6. Just before serving, garnish with fresh parsley that has been chopped.

91.   SPICY OKRA AND POTATO HASH

Total Time: 45 minutes

Prep Time: 15 minutes

Ingredients:

- 2 cups okra, sliced
- 2 cups potatoes, diced
- 1 onion, chopped
- 1 bell pepper, diced
- 2 cloves garlic, minced
- 2 tablespoons Cajun seasoning
- 1 teaspoon smoked paprika
- Salt and pepper to taste
- 3 tablespoons olive oil
- Fresh thyme, chopped (for garnish)

Directions:

1. Get the olive oil ready by warming it in a big pan on medium heat. Include the bell pepper, potatoes, onions, and garlic in the dish. To get a golden brown color, sauté the potatoes.
2. Cajun spice, smoked paprika, sliced okra, salt, and pepper should be stirred in at this point. Allow the okra to cook until it is soft but retains a small crunch.
3. When necessary, adjust the seasoning. Fresh thyme should be used as a garnish before serving.

92.   CAJUN BLACK BEAN AND RICE BURRITOS

Total Time: 30 minutes

Prep Time: 15 minutes

Ingredients:

- 1 cup cooked black beans
- 1 cup cooked rice
- 1 bell pepper, diced
- 1/2 cup corn kernels
- 1/4 cup red onion, finely chopped
- 2 tablespoons tomato paste
- 1 tablespoon Cajun seasoning

- 1 teaspoon cumin
- 4 large whole-grain tortillas
- Vegan cheese, shredded (optional)
- Fresh cilantro, chopped (for garnish)
- Lime wedges (for serving)

Directions:

1. The following ingredients should be combined in a bowl: black beans, rice, bell pepper, corn, red onion, tomato paste, cumin, and Cajun spice.
2. Place a portion of the mixture on each tortilla, and if you so choose, sprinkle it with vegan cheese. Then, fold the tortillas into burritos.
3. Burritos should be cooked in a pan that has been heated over medium heat until they are golden brown on all sides.
4. The dish should be served with lime wedges and garnished with fresh cilantro.

93.   VEGAN ANDOUILLE SAUSAGE

Total Time: 1 hour 30 minutes

Prep Time: 30 minutes

Ingredients:

- 1 cup vital wheat gluten
- 1/4 cup nutritional yeast
- 2 tablespoons smoked paprika
- 1 tablespoon fennel seeds, crushed
- 1 teaspoon garlic powder
- 1 teaspoon onion powder
- 1/2 teaspoon cayenne pepper
- 1/2 cup vegetable broth
- 2 tablespoons soy sauce
- 1 tablespoon olive oil

Directions:

1. The essential wheat gluten, nutritional yeast, smoked paprika, fennel seeds, garlic powder, onion powder, and cayenne pepper should be mixed together in a big bowl.
2. Place the olive oil, soy sauce, and vegetable broth in a separate bowl and stir them together.
3. Knead the mixture until dough forms after adding the liquid components to the dry ingredients.
4. Make sections of the dough that are about the size of sausages, and then wrap each one in aluminum foil.
5. Forty-five minutes should be spent steaming the sausages.
6. Remove the wrapping and fry the food in a skillet until it has browned. Use in the meals that you enjoy the most!

94.   CREOLE-STYLE STUFFED BELL PEPPERS

Total Time: 1 hour 15 minutes

Prep Time: 30 minutes

Ingredients:

- 4 large bell peppers, halved and seeds removed
- 1 cup cooked quinoa
- 1 can black beans, drained and rinsed
- 1 cup corn kernels
- 1 cup diced tomatoes
- 1/2 cup diced red onion
- 1/4 cup chopped fresh parsley
- 2 cloves garlic, minced
- 1 teaspoon cumin
- 1 teaspoon paprika
- Salt and pepper to taste
- 1 cup tomato sauce

Directions:

1. Bake at 375 F (190 C) for at least 10 minutes.
2. All of the following ingredients should be mixed together in a big bowl: quinoa, black beans, corn, tomatoes, red onion, parsley, garlic, cumin, paprika, salt, and pepper.
3. Prepare a baking dish and fill each half of a bell pepper with the quinoa mixture. Place the peppers in the dish.
4. Over the peppers that have been filled, pour tomato sauce.
5. Place the foil on top, and bake for forty-five minutes. Bake for a further fifteen minutes after removing the lid.
6. The dish should be served hot and garnished with more parsley.

95.   DIRTY RICE AND BLACK BEAN TOSTADAS

Total Time: 45 minutes

Prep Time: 20 minutes

Ingredients:

- 1 cup brown rice, cooked
- 1 can black beans, mashed
- 1 cup diced bell peppers (any color)
- 1 cup diced red onion
- 2 cloves garlic, minced
- 1 teaspoon Cajun seasoning
- 1/2 teaspoon thyme
- Salt and pepper to taste
- 8 tostada shells
- 1 avocado, sliced
- Lime wedges for serving

Directions:

1. To soften the bell peppers, red onion, and garlic, sauté them in a pan until they are tender.
2. Cajun seasoning, thyme, salt, and pepper should be added to the mashed black beans and rice that has been cooked. Continue to cook until the food is completely heated.
3. Heat the tostada shells in accordance with the instructions on the box.
4. Place a dollop of the mixture consisting of filthy rice and black beans onto each tostada shell.
5. To finish, garnish with sliced avocado and serve with slices of lime.

96.   CAJUN-STYLE CUCUMBER SALAD

Total Time: 15 minutes

Prep Time: 10 minutes

Ingredients:

- 2 large cucumbers, thinly sliced
- 1 red bell pepper, diced
- 1/2 red onion, thinly sliced
- 1/4 cup fresh parsley, chopped
- 1/4 cup olive oil
- 2 tablespoons apple cider vinegar

- 1 teaspoon Cajun seasoning
- 1/2 teaspoon garlic powder
- Salt and black pepper to taste
- 1 tablespoon fresh lemon juice (optional)

Directions:

1. Coat the cucumbers that have been sliced, the red bell pepper that has been diced, the red onion that has been finely sliced, and the chopped parsley in a large basin.
2. The olive oil, apple cider vinegar, Cajun spice, garlic powder, salt, and black pepper should be mixed together in a small basin. Stir in order to combine.
3. Once the dressing has been poured over the cucumber mixture, toss it until it is thoroughly incorporated.
4. Take the salad and marinate it for at least five minutes so that the flavors may combine and become more pronounced. Squeeze in some fresh lemon juice right before serving to give the salad even more brightness.
5. Prepare the Cajun-style cucumber Salad in the refrigerator and serve it as a light appetizer or as a refreshing side dish.

97.   SPICY TOFU BOUDIN BALLS

Total Time: 45 minutes

Prep Time: 20 minutes

Ingredients:

- 1 block extra-firm tofu, pressed and crumbled
- 1 cup cooked brown rice
- 1/2 cup finely diced onion
- 1/4 cup finely diced celery
- 2 cloves garlic, minced
- 1 tablespoon Cajun seasoning
- 1 teaspoon paprika
- 1/2 teaspoon thyme
- 1/4 teaspoon cayenne pepper
- Salt and pepper to taste
- 1 cup breadcrumbs
- Oil for frying

Directions:

1. Tofu that has been crushed, rice that has been cooked, onion, celery, garlic, Cajun spice, paprika, thyme, cayenne pepper, salt, and pepper should be mixed together in a big bowl.
2. The mixture should be formed into balls about the size of golf balls, and then the balls should be covered with breadcrumbs.
3. In a skillet, bring the oil to a setting of medium heat. The tofu balls should be fried until they are golden brown and crispy.
4. The excess oil should be absorbed by placing the removed item on paper towels. Serve warm with your preferred dipping sauce on the side.

98.   VEGAN DIRTY RICE RISOTTO

Total Time: 50 minutes

Prep Time: 15 minutes

Ingredients:

- 1 cup Arborio rice
- 1/2 cup finely diced onion
- 1/4 cup finely diced bell pepper
- 1/4 cup finely diced celery
- 2 cloves garlic, minced
- 1 cup vegan sausage, crumbled

- 1 tablespoon Cajun seasoning
- 4 cups vegetable broth, heated
- 1/2 cup dry white wine (optional)
- Salt and pepper to taste
- Chopped green onions for garnish

Directions:

1. Sauté the onion, bell pepper, celery, and garlic in a large pan until the vegetables have become more tender.
2. Include rice, Cajun spice, and vegan sausage in the dish. Continue cooking the rice while tossing it frequently until it is evenly covered and has a toasted flavor.
3. Transfer the wine to the pan and heat it until most of the alcohol is absorbed.
4. When adding the hot vegetable broth, start by adding one ladle at a time, swirling the mixture regularly until all of the liquid has been absorbed before trying to add more.
5. Continue doing this until the rice reaches the desired consistency and is cooked to your satisfaction. Use pepper and salt to season the food.
6. Prior to serving, garnish with green onions that have been chopped.

99.   CAJUN-STYLE VEGAN CORN CHOWDER

Total Time: 40 minutes

Prep Time: 15 minutes

Ingredients:

- 2 tablespoons olive oil
- 1 onion, diced
- 2 bell peppers, diced
- 3 cloves garlic, minced
- 4 cups corn kernels (fresh or frozen)

- 4 cups vegetable broth
- 1 can (14 oz) coconut milk
- 1 teaspoon Cajun seasoning
- 1/2 teaspoon smoked paprika
- Salt and pepper to taste
- Fresh parsley for garnish

Directions:

1. In a big saucepan, bring the olive oil to a boil and keep it there. The garlic, onion, and bell peppers should be added. For veggies to become more tender, sauté them.
2. Cajun seasoning, smoked paprika, salt, and pepper should be added to the mixture along with corn. Allow to come to a simmer.
3. Allow it to boil and stir it occasionally for twenty to twenty-five minutes.
4. If it is required, adjust the seasoning. Serve while still hot, with fresh parsley as a garnish.

100. CAJUN COLLARD GREEN AND QUINOA SALAD

Total Time: 30 minutes

Prep Time: 15 minutes

Ingredients:

- 1 cup quinoa, cooked and cooled
- 4 cups chopped fresh collard greens
- 1 bell pepper, diced
- 1 cup cherry tomatoes, halved
- 1/4 cup red onion, finely chopped

- 1/4 cup chopped fresh parsley
- 1/4 cup olive oil
- 2 tablespoons apple cider vinegar
- 1 teaspoon Dijon mustard
- 1 teaspoon Cajun seasoning
- Salt and pepper to taste

Directions:

1. Before serving, quickly mix the quinoa with the bell pepper, parsley, red onion, cherry tomatoes, and collard leaves.
2. For the Cajun seasoning, in a small bowl, combine the olive oil, Dijon mustard, apple cider vinegar, salt, and pepper. Whisk gently to combine.
3. After pouring the dressing over the salad, mix it to integrate the flavors.
4. Before serving, place the dish in the refrigerator for at least fifteen minutes to enable the flavors to combine. To be served cold.

101. VEGAN MARDI GRAS TOSTADAS

Total Time: 30 minutes

Prep Time: 15 minutes

Ingredients:

- 8 small corn tortillas
- 1 cup canned black beans, drained and rinsed
- 1 cup diced tomatoes
- 1 cup shredded purple cabbage
- 1 avocado, sliced
- 1/2 cup corn kernels
- 1/4 cup chopped fresh cilantro
- Lime wedges for serving

Directions:

1. Bring the temperature of the oven up to 175 degrees Celsius (350 degrees Fahrenheit).
2. Cook the tortillas for five to seven minutes, or until they reach the desired level of crispiness, on a baking sheet.
3. Put the black beans, tomatoes, cabbage, avocado, corn, and cilantro into a bowl and mix them together.
4. Transfer the mixture to each tortilla using a spoon.
5. Lime wedges should be served on the side accompanying the tostadas.

102.   BLACKENED TEMPEH CAESAR SALAD BOWL

Total Time: 45 minutes

Prep Time: 20 minutes

Ingredients:

- 1 package (8 oz) tempeh, sliced
- 1 tablespoon Cajun seasoning
- 6 cups chopped romaine lettuce
- 1 cup cherry tomatoes, halved
- 1/2 cup vegan Caesar dressing
- 1/4 cup nutritional yeast
- 1/4 cup croutons (optional)

Directions:

1. Applying Cajun flavor to the tempeh slices is a good idea.
2. The tempeh should be cooked in a pan over medium heat for three to four minutes on each side until it has a charred appearance.
3. The romaine lettuce, cherry tomatoes, and tempeh that have been charred should be mixed together in a big dish.
4. Use a drizzle of Caesar dressing, sprinkle some nutritional yeast on top, and mix everything together.
5. Croutons can be sprinkled on top if desired.

103. CREOLE-STYLE ZUCCHINI NOODLES

Total Time: 25 minutes

Prep Time: 15 minutes

Ingredients:

- 4 medium zucchinis, spiralized
- 1 tablespoon olive oil
- 1 onion, finely chopped
- 2 bell peppers, diced
- 3 cloves garlic, minced

- 1 can (14 oz) diced tomatoes
- 1 teaspoon Cajun seasoning
- Salt and pepper to taste
- Fresh parsley for garnish

Directions:

1. Melt the olive oil in a big saucepan over medium heat.
2. The garlic, onions, and bell peppers should be added. To soften the meat, sauté it.
3. For three to five minutes, until the zucchini is cooked, add spiralized zucchini to the pan and cook it.
4. Cajun spice and chopped tomatoes should be added right now. Cook for a further five minutes after giving it a thorough stir.
5. Before seasoning with salt, add pepper and salt to taste.
6. Immediately prior to serving, garnish with fresh parsley.

104.   CREOLE LENTIL AND SWEET POTATO CURRY

Total Time: 40 minutes

Prep Time: 20 minutes

Ingredients:

- 1 cup dried green lentils, rinsed
- 2 sweet potatoes, peeled and diced
- 1 can (14 oz) coconut milk
- 1 onion, finely chopped
- 3 cloves garlic, minced
- 1 tablespoon Creole seasoning
- 1 teaspoon ground cumin
- 1 teaspoon ground coriander
- Salt and pepper to taste
- Fresh cilantro for garnish

Directions:

1. Put the lentils, sweet potatoes, coconut milk, onion, garlic, Creole spice, cumin, and coriander into a saucepan and mix them together.
2. Once the lentils and sweet potatoes have reached the desired tenderness, bring them to a boil, then decrease the heat and simmer for twenty to twenty-five minutes.
3. Before seasoning with salt, add pepper and salt to taste.
4. Fresh cilantro should be used as a garnish before serving.

105.　DIRTY RICE-STUFFED ACORN SQUASH

Total Time: 1 hour 30 minutes

Prep Time: 30 minutes

Ingredients:

- 2 acorn squashes, halved, and seeds removed
- 1 cup brown rice, cooked
- 1 cup vegan sausage, crumbled
- 1 onion, finely chopped
- 1 bell pepper, diced
- 2 celery stalks, finely chopped
- 3 cloves garlic, minced
- 1 teaspoon Cajun seasoning
- 1 teaspoon thyme
- Salt and pepper to taste
- 2 tablespoons olive oil
- Green onions for garnish

Directions:

1. Position the oven dial to 375 °F, which is equivalent to 190 °C.
2. Transfer the halved acorn squash halves, cut side down, to a baking pan.
3. Make sure that the olive oil is brought to a simmer in a big saucepan that is set over medium heat before it is used.
4. Include garlic, onion, bell pepper, and celery in the mixture. To soften the meat, sauté it.
5. To the skillet, add crumbled vegan sausage and heat it until it has a browned appearance.
6. Rice that has been cooked, Cajun spice, thyme, salt, and pepper should be stirred in. Combine thoroughly.
7. Place a portion of the rice and sausage mixture inside of each half of the acorn squash.
8. Bake in an oven that has been warmed for forty-five to fifty minutes or until the squash is soft.
9. Prior to serving, garnish with green onions that have been chopped.

106. CAJUN STUFFED MUSHROOMS

Total Time: 45 minutes

Prep Time: 20 minutes

Ingredients:

- 20 large mushrooms, cleaned and stems removed
- 1 cup breadcrumbs
- 1 cup spinach, chopped
- 1/2 cup vegan cream cheese
- 1 onion, finely diced
- 2 cloves garlic, minced
- 1 teaspoon Cajun seasoning
- Salt and pepper to taste
- 2 tablespoons olive oil
- Fresh parsley for garnish

Directions:

1. Get the oven hot, about 190 degrees Celsius (375 degrees Fahrenheit).
2. Cook the olive oil in a saucepan on a medium heat setting.
3. Sauté the onion and garlic until they have become more tame.
4. When the spinach has become wilted, add it to the skillet and continue to cook it.
5. Breadcrumbs, vegan cream cheese, Cajun spice, salt, pepper, and the spinach combination that has been sautéed should be mixed together first in a bowl.
6. The mushroom caps should be placed on a baking sheet, and the mixture should be neatly stuffed into each mushroom cap.
7. To ensure that the mushrooms are soft, bake them for 25 to 30 minutes.
8. Immediately prior to serving, garnish with fresh parsley.

107. DIRTY RICE AND BLACK BEAN BURRITOS

Total Time: 40 minutes

Prep Time: 15 minutes

Ingredients:

- 1 cup brown rice, cooked
- 1 can black beans, drained and rinsed
- 1 cup vegan sausage, crumbled
- 1 onion, diced
- 1 bell pepper, sliced
- 2 cloves garlic, minced
- 1 teaspoon Cajun seasoning
- 1 teaspoon cumin
- Salt and pepper to taste
- Flour tortillas
- Avocado slices and salsa for serving

Directions:

1. Cook the olive oil in a saucepan on a medium heat setting. Garlic, onion, and bell pepper should be added. To soften the meat, sauté it.
2. When it is browned, add crumbled vegan sausage and continue to cook.
3. Rice that has been cooked, black beans, Cajun spice, cumin, salt, and pepper should be stirred in. Combine thoroughly.
4. Before placing the rice and sausage mixture on each flour tortilla, warm the tortillas and spread it out with a spoon.
5. The tortillas should be rolled into burritos, and they should be served with pieces of avocado and salsa.

108. VEGAN MAQUE CHOUX TOSTADAS

Total Time: 35 minutes

Prep Time: 20 minutes

Ingredients:

- 4 tostada shells
- 2 cups corn kernels (fresh or frozen)
- 1 bell pepper, diced
- 1 cup cherry tomatoes, halved
- 1 jalapeño, finely chopped
- 1/2 cup red onion, finely chopped

- 2 cloves garlic, minced
- 1 teaspoon Cajun seasoning
- 1/2 teaspoon smoked paprika
- 2 tablespoons lime juice
- Fresh cilantro for garnish
- Vegan sour cream for topping

Directions:

1. Cook the olive oil in a saucepan on a medium heat setting.
2. Add garlic, red onion, and bell pepper to the mixture. To soften the meat, sauté it.
3. Cajun seasoning, smoked paprika, corn, cherry tomatoes, jalapeño, and lime juice should be added to the mixture. For ten to twelve minutes, cook.
4. Put the tostada shells on a dish that is intended for serving.
5. Tostada shells should be topped with the Maque Choux mixture using a spoon.
6. Just before serving, garnish with fresh cilantro and a dollop of vegan sour cream.

109. CAJUN CHICKPEA CREPES

Total Time: 45 minutes

Prep Time: 15 minutes

Servings: 4

Ingredients:

- 1 cup chickpea flour
- 1 1/2 cups water
- 1 tablespoon olive oil
- 1 teaspoon Cajun seasoning
- 1/2 teaspoon salt
- 1/4 cup chopped green onions
- 1/4 cup diced tomatoes
- 1/4 cup sliced bell peppers
- Cooking spray

Directions:

1. In a bowl, combine chickpea flour, water, olive oil, Cajun seasoning, and salt by whisking them together until they are completely smooth. Ten minutes should be allowed for the batter to rest.
2. A non-stick skillet should be heated over medium heat and then lightly coated with cooking spray before being used.
3. After pouring a quarter cup of the batter into the skillet, swirl it around to ensure that it is distributed evenly. During the first two to three minutes of cooking, the edges should begin to lift.
4. One-half of the crepe should be topped with a garnish consisting of green onions, tomatoes, and bell peppers. Over the vegetables, fold the remaining half of the dough.
5. After cooking for an additional two minutes, flip the food and continue cooking for an additional one to two minutes or until it reaches a golden brown color.
6. Proceed in the same manner with the remaining batter and filling. Cajun chickpea crepes should be served warm, and you should enjoy them.

110. SPICY GUMBO GREENS

Total Time: 30 minutes

Prep Time: 10 minutes

Servings: 6

Ingredients:

- 1 lb mixed greens (collard, mustard, kale), chopped
- 1 onion, finely chopped
- 3 cloves garlic, minced
- 1 bell pepper, diced
- 1 cup okra, sliced

- 1 can (15 oz) diced tomatoes
- 4 cups vegetable broth
- 2 teaspoons Cajun seasoning
- 1/2 teaspoon hot sauce
- Salt and pepper to taste
- Cooked rice for serving

Directions:

1. The onions, garlic, and bell pepper should be sautéed in a big saucepan until they become more tender.
2. Cajun seasoning, spicy sauce, chopped greens, diced tomatoes, diced okra, diced tomatoes, vegetable broth, and salt and pepper should be added.
3. The greens should be cooked until they are soft, which should take twenty minutes. Bring to a simmer.
4. Adjust the seasoning to your liking. While the rice is cooking, serve. Spicy Gumbo Greens, I hope you enjoy these!

111. VEGAN SHRIMP CREOLE

Total Time: 40 minutes

Prep Time: 15 minutes

Servings: 4

Ingredients:

- 1 lb vegan shrimp, thawed
- 1 onion, diced
- 2 bell peppers, diced
- 3 cloves garlic, minced
- 1 can (15 oz) crushed tomatoes
- 1/2 cup vegetable broth

- 2 tablespoons tomato paste
- 1 tablespoon Cajun seasoning
- 1 teaspoon hot sauce
- Salt and pepper to taste
- Cooked rice for serving

Directions:

1. To soften the onion, bell peppers, and garlic, sauté them in a pan until they are tender.
2. After adding vegan shrimp, continue to simmer for another three to four minutes until the shrimp are completely cooked.
3. Add crushed tomatoes, tomato paste, vegetable broth, Cajun spice, spicy sauce, salt, and pepper to the mixture and stir to combine.
4. In order for the flavors to combine, simmer for twenty minutes. When necessary, adjust the seasoning.
5. While the rice is cooking, serve. Wishing you a delicious vegan shrimp creole!

112. VEGAN RED BEANS AND AVOCADO TOAST

Total Time: 25 minutes

Prep Time: 10 minutes

Servings: 2

Ingredients:

- 1 can (15 oz) red kidney beans, drained and rinsed
- 1/2 onion, finely chopped
- 2 cloves garlic, minced
- 1 teaspoon Cajun seasoning
- 1 avocado, mashed
- 4 slices whole-grain bread, toasted
- Lemon wedges for garnish
- Salt and pepper to taste

Directions:

1. Sauté the onions and garlic in a skillet until the onions become transparent. Cajun spice and red beans should be added. 5-7 minutes of cooking time.
2. Toasted bread pieces should be covered with the avocado that has been mashed.
3. Spread the red bean mixture on top of the bread topped with avocado.
4. Salt and pepper should be sprinkled on top. Each toast should have a lemon slice squeezed over it.
5. Enjoy your Vegan Red Beans and Avocado Toast as soon as possible and serve it to your guests.

113. VEGAN MARDI GRAS KING CAKE

Total Time: 2 hours

Prep Time: 30 minutes

Ingredients:

- 1 cup almond milk, warmed
- 1 packet of active dry yeast
- 1/4 cup sugar
- 1/4 cup vegan butter, melted
- 1/2 teaspoon vanilla extract
- 3 1/2 cups all-purpose flour
- 1/2 teaspoon salt
- 1/2 cup unsweetened applesauce

- 1/2 cup chopped pecans
- 1/2 cup raisins
- 1 tablespoon ground cinnamon
- 1/4 cup powdered sugar (for glaze)
- Purple, green, and yellow natural food coloring

Directions:

1. The yeast, sugar, and warm almond milk should be mixed together in a bowl. For five minutes, let it sit until it becomes frothy.
2. Mix in some melted vegan butter, some vanilla essence, some flour, some salt, and some applesauce. To make a dough, continue to mix.
3. For five minutes, knead the dough on a surface that has been dusted with flour. Cover it with a greased bowl, and let it aside for an hour to rise.
4. Spread the cinnamon, pecans, and raisins over the dough before rolling it out. Form it into a circle by rolling it into a log and shaping it.
5. The recommended baking time is 25 to 30 minutes at 350 F (175 C).
6. After the glaze has cooled, split it into three dishes, add some food coloring to each bowl, and then pour it over the cake.

114. JAZZY JACKFRUIT TACOS WITH LIME CREMA

Total Time: 45 minutes

Prep Time: 15 minutes

Ingredients:

- 2 cans of young jackfruit, drained and shredded
- 2 tablespoons Cajun seasoning
- 1 tablespoon olive oil
- 1 onion, diced
- 2 cloves garlic, minced
- 1 bell pepper, thinly sliced
- 8 small tortillas
- Shredded lettuce
- Sliced tomatoes
- Lime crema (1/2 cup vegan sour cream + juice of 1 lime)

Directions:

1. Cajun spice should be tossed with jackfruit. In olive oil, sauté the onion and garlic until they become tender.
2. Cook the jackfruit and bell pepper until the jackfruit is tender. Add the jackfruit.
3. Tacos that are warm. Incorporate lettuce, tomatoes, and jackfruit mixture into the filling.
4. Crema may be made by combining vegan sour cream and lime juice. Pour over tacos and serve.

115. SPICY CAJUN CAULIFLOWER BITES

Total Time: 40 minutes

Prep Time: 15 minutes

Ingredients:

- 1 head cauliflower, cut into florets
- 1 cup chickpea flour
- 1 cup water
- 1 tablespoon Cajun seasoning
- 1 teaspoon garlic powder
- 1/2 teaspoon smoked paprika
- Salt and pepper to taste
- Olive oil for baking

Directions:

1. Turn the oven on high heat (around 220 degrees Celsius, or 425 degrees Fahrenheit).
2. For the batter, combine chickpea flour, water, Cajun spice, garlic powder, smoked paprika, salt, and pepper by whisking all of the ingredients together.
3. Prepare a baking sheet and arrange cauliflower florets on it after dipping them in batter.
4. Bake for twenty-five to thirty minutes, drizzling with olive oil, until the crust is crunchy.

116. RED PEPPER AND ARTICHOKE TOSTADAS

Total Time: 30 minutes

Prep Time: 15 minutes

Ingredients:

- 8 tostada shells
- 1 can (14 oz) artichoke hearts, drained and chopped
- 1 cup roasted red peppers, sliced
- 1 cup cherry tomatoes, halved
- 1/2 cup red onion, finely chopped
- 1/4 cup fresh cilantro, chopped
- 1 avocado, sliced
- Cajun-inspired dressing (olive oil, hot sauce, garlic, lemon juice)

Directions:

1. Prepare a serving tray and arrange the tostada shells on it.
2. Artichoke hearts, red peppers, cherry tomatoes, red onion, and cilantro should all be mixed together in a bowl.
3. Transfer the mixture to each tostada shell using a spoon.
4. Place slices of avocado on top, then drizzle with a dressing that is influenced by Cajun cuisine.

117. VEGAN JAMBALAYA STUFFED ZUCCHINI

Total Time: 45 minutes

Prep Time: 15 minutes

Ingredients:

- 4 large zucchinis
- 1 cup brown rice, cooked
- 1 cup diced tomatoes
- 1 cup bell peppers, diced
- 1 cup black beans, cooked
- 1 cup corn kernels
- 1 onion, finely chopped
- 3 cloves garlic, minced
- 1 teaspoon Cajun seasoning
- 1 teaspoon paprika
- Salt and pepper to taste
- 2 tablespoons olive oil
- Fresh parsley for garnish

Directions:

1. Get the oven up to 375 °F or 190 °C.)
2. The zucchini should be cut in half lengthwise, and the core should be scooped out, leaving behind a structure that resembles a boat.
3. The onions and garlic should be cooked in olive oil in a skillet until they become transparent.
4. Incorporate maize, tomatoes, bell peppers, and black beans into the dish. Allow veggies to cook until they are soft.
5. Rice that has been cooked, Cajun seasoning, paprika, salt, and pepper should be stirred in.
6. Stuff the rice and veggie mixture into each zucchini boat that you have prepared.
7. Bake the stuffed zucchini for twenty-five to thirty minutes after placing them on a baking sheet.
8. Immediately prior to serving, garnish with fresh parsley.

118. VEGAN SAUSAGE GUMBO

Total Time: 1 hour

Prep Time: 20 minutes

Ingredients:

- 1 cup vegan sausage, sliced
- 1/2 cup flour
- 1/2 cup vegetable oil
- 1 onion, diced
- 1 bell pepper, diced
- 2 celery stalks, chopped
- 3 cloves garlic, minced

- 1 can okra, sliced
- 1 can diced tomatoes
- 4 cups vegetable broth
- 1 teaspoon thyme
- 1 teaspoon Cajun seasoning
- Salt and pepper to taste
- Cooked rice for serving

Directions:

1. The flour and vegetable oil should be mixed together in a big saucepan and heated over medium heat to create a roux. Never stop stirring it until it reaches a rich brown color.
2. Include garlic, onions, bell peppers, and celery in the mixture. To ensure that the veggies are cooked through.
3. Incorporate the following Ingredients: vegan sausage, chopped tomatoes, diced okra, thyme, Cajun spice, salt, and pepper.
4. Incorporate the vegetable broth into the mixture and bring it to a boil before adding it. Cook for thirty to forty minutes.
5. While the rice is cooking, serve.

119.   CAJUN QUINOA-STUFFED BELL PEPPER SOUP

Total Time: 40 minutes

Prep Time: 15 minutes

Ingredients:

- 4 bell peppers, halved
- 1 cup quinoa, cooked
- 1 can black beans, drained and rinsed
- 1 cup corn kernels
- 1 onion, diced
- 3 cloves garlic, minced
- 1 can diced tomatoes
- 4 cups vegetable broth
- 1 teaspoon Cajun seasoning
- Salt and pepper to taste
- Chopped green onions for garnish

Directions:

1. Get the oven up to 375 °F or 190 °C.)
2. The bell pepper halves should be roasted for fifteen minutes after being placed on a baking pan.
3. Sauté the onions and garlic in a large saucepan until the onions become transparent.
4. Incorporate Cajun seasoning, black beans, corn, chopped tomatoes, quinoa that has been cooked, and salt & pepper to taste. Cook for a period of five minutes.
5. The soup should be brought to a simmer once the vegetable broth has been added. Continue cooking for five to twenty minutes more.
6. Place the quinoa mixture inside of each bell pepper that has been roasted.
7. Prior to serving, garnish with green onions that have been chopped.

120. CAJUN CHICKPEA AND SPINACH CURRY

Total Time: 30 minutes

Prep Time: 10 minutes

Ingredients:

- 1 can chickpeas, drained and rinsed
- 1 onion, finely chopped
- 3 cloves garlic, minced
- 1 cup diced tomatoes
- 2 cups fresh spinach

- 1 can of coconut milk
- 1 tablespoon Cajun seasoning
- 1 teaspoon cumin
- 1 teaspoon paprika
- Salt and pepper to taste
- Cooked rice for serving

Directions:

1. Bring the garlic and onions to a simmer in a skillet until they soften.
2. Chickpeas, chopped tomatoes, Cajun spice, cumin, paprika, salt, and pepper should be added to the mixture. Cook for a period of five minutes.
3. After adding the coconut milk, continue to boil for ten more minutes if necessary.
4. In a pan, soften the garlic and onions by simmering them.
5. While the rice is cooking, serve.

121. VEGAN JAMBALAYA RISOTTO

Total Time: 40 minutes

Prep Time: 15 minutes

Serves: 4

Ingredients:

- 1 cup Arborio rice
- 1 onion, finely chopped
- 1 bell pepper, diced
- 2 celery stalks, chopped
- 1 cup cherry tomatoes, halved
- 1 cup okra, sliced
- 3 cloves garlic, minced
- 1 tablespoon Cajun seasoning
- 4 cups vegetable broth
- 1 can (15 oz) kidney beans, drained and rinsed
- Salt and pepper to taste
- Green onions for garnish

Directions:

1. The onions, bell pepper, and celery should be sautéed in a big pan until they become tender.
2. After two minutes of stirring, proceed to add the garlic and Arborio rice.
3. Before adding extra vegetable broth, whisk in the Cajun seasoning and add a little at a time, about one cup at a time, allowing the liquid to soak.
4. After adding the kidney beans, okra, and cherry tomatoes, continue stirring the rice until it reaches a creamy consistency and is cooked.
5. Before seasoning with salt, add pepper and salt to taste.
6. Green onions should be used as a garnish before serving.

122. QUINOA-STUFFED MIRLITON BOATS

Total Time: 50 minutes

Prep Time: 20 minutes

Serves: 6

Ingredients:

- 3 mirlitons (chayotes), halved and seeds removed
- 1 cup quinoa, cooked
- 1 can (15 oz) black beans, drained and rinsed
- 1 cup corn kernels
- 1 red onion, finely chopped
- 1 jalapeño, minced
- 1 teaspoon cumin
- 1 teaspoon paprika
- Salt and pepper to taste
- Fresh cilantro for garnish

Directions:

1. Bake at a temperature of 190 degrees Celsius (375 degrees Fahrenheit).
2. When the mirliton halves have been boiled for fifteen minutes, scoop off a portion of the meat to create boats.
3. Combine cooked quinoa, black beans, corn, red onion, jalapeño, cumin, paprika, salt, and pepper in a bowl. Mix well the ingredients together.
4. Place a little of the quinoa mixture inside of each mirliton boat.
5. To ensure that the mirliton is soft, bake it for twenty-five minutes.
6. Fresh cilantro should be used as a garnish before serving.

123. SPICY VEGAN CAJUN PASTA

Total Time: 30 minutes

Prep Time: 15 minutes

Serves: 4

Ingredients:

- 8 oz linguine or your preferred pasta
- 1 tablespoon olive oil
- 1 onion, thinly sliced
- 1 bell pepper, thinly sliced
- 1 cup mushrooms, sliced
- 3 cloves garlic, minced
- 1 can (14 oz) diced tomatoes
- 1 teaspoon Cajun seasoning
- 1/2 teaspoon red pepper flakes (adjust to taste)
- Salt and pepper to taste
- Fresh parsley for garnish

Directions:

1. Pasta should be cooked according to package recommendations.
2. Olive oil should be used to sauté onions, bell peppers, mushrooms, and garlic in a big skillet until the vegetables become more tender.
3. Red pepper flakes, chopped tomatoes, and Cajun seasoning should be added to the dish. Let it simmer for ten minutes.
4. Put the cooked pasta into the sauce and make sure it is evenly coated with the sauce.
5. Use pepper and salt to season the food. Immediately prior to serving, garnish with fresh parsley.

124. VEGAN MARDI GRAS NACHOS

Total Time: 25 minutes

Prep Time: 15 minutes

Serves: 4

Ingredients:

- 1 bag tortilla chips
- 1 can (15 oz) black beans, mashed
- 1 cup vegan cheese, shredded
- 1 cup cherry tomatoes, diced
- 1/2 cup black olives, sliced

- 1 avocado, diced
- 1/4 cup pickled jalapeños
- Vegan sour cream for topping
- Fresh cilantro for garnish

Directions:

1. Bring the temperature of the oven up to 175 degrees Celsius (350 degrees Fahrenheit).
2. Place tortilla chips in a single layer on a baking sheet.
3. The chips should be covered with mashed black beans, and vegan cheese should be sprinkled on top.
4. Cherry tomatoes, black olives, chopped avocado, and pickled jalapeños are the toppings that should be added.
5. Baking time should be ten minutes or until the cheese has melted.
6. As soon as it is removed from the oven, sprinkle it with vegan sour cream. Serve with a garnish of fresh cilantro.

125.   CREOLE EGGPLANT STIR-FRY

Total Time: 25 minutes

Prep Time: 10 minutes

Ingredients:

- 1 large eggplant, cubed
- 1 red bell pepper, sliced
- 1 yellow bell pepper, sliced
- 1 cup cherry tomatoes, halved
- 1 onion, thinly sliced
- 3 cloves garlic, minced
- 2 tablespoons soy sauce
- 1 tablespoon Creole seasoning
- 2 tablespoons olive oil
- Salt and pepper to taste
- Fresh parsley for garnish

Directions:

1. Take a pan and place it over medium heat. Warm the olive oil. Sauté the garlic and onion until they have become more tender.
2. You should also include cherry tomatoes, bell peppers, and eggplant. Cook the veggies until they are cooked but can still be crunchy.
3. Add the Creole seasoning, soy sauce, salt, and pepper, and stir to combine. Continue to cook for an additional three to five minutes.
4. Add some fresh parsley as a garnish, and serve the dish over quinoa or rice.

126. VEGAN MUFFULETTA PASTA BAKE

Total Time: 45 minutes

Prep Time: 15 minutes

Ingredients:

- 1 lb pasta of your choice
- 1 can (14 oz) artichoke hearts, drained and chopped
- 1 cup green olives, sliced
- 1 cup black olives, sliced
- 1 cup cherry tomatoes, halved
- 1 cup vegan mozzarella, shredded
- 1/2 cup fresh basil, chopped
- 1/4 cup olive oil
- 2 cloves garlic, minced
- Salt and pepper to taste

Directions:

1. I will start by getting the oven preheated to 190 degrees Celsius, which is 375 degrees Fahrenheit.
2. Set the pasta aside to cook as directed on the package.
3. Artichoke hearts, olives, cherry tomatoes, vegan mozzarella, and basil should be mixed together in a big bowl.
4. To start, heat a small pan over medium heat and sauté the garlic until it starts to smell good.
5. After pouring over the pasta mixture, toss it to ensure that it is evenly coated.
6. When you have transferred the mixture to a baking dish, bake it for twenty-five to thirty minutes or until it is bubbling and golden, whichever comes first.

127. CAJUN-STYLE VEGAN COLESLAW

Total Time: 15 minutes

Prep Time: 15 minutes

Ingredients:

- 1 small green cabbage, finely shredded
- 1 carrot, grated
- 1 red bell pepper, finely sliced
- 1/2 cup vegan mayonnaise

- 2 tablespoons Dijon mustard
- 1 tablespoon apple cider vinegar
- 1 teaspoon Cajun seasoning
- Salt and pepper to taste
- Fresh parsley for garnish

Directions:

1. Put the shredded cabbage, grated carrot, and sliced bell pepper into a big bowl and mix things together.
2. Another bowl should be used to combine vegan mayonnaise, Dijon mustard, apple cider vinegar, Cajun spice, salt, and pepper. Whisk all of these ingredients together.
3. Pouring the dressing over the vegetables and tossing them will guarantee that they are not only coated but also covered evenly.
4. Apply a garnish of fresh parsley, and place the dish in the refrigerator for at least half an hour before serving.

128. VEGAN ZYDECO ZOODLES

Total Time: 20 minutes

Prep Time: 10 minutes

Ingredients:

- 4 medium zucchinis, spiralized
- 1 can (15 oz) black beans, drained and rinsed
- 1 cup corn kernels (fresh or frozen)
- 1 red onion, finely diced
- 2 cloves garlic, minced
- 2 tablespoons Cajun seasoning
- 2 tablespoons lime juice
- 2 tablespoons olive oil
- Salt and pepper to taste
- Fresh cilantro for garnish

Directions:

1. Take a pan and place it over medium heat. Warm the olive oil.
2. Sauté the garlic and red onion till they have become more tender.
3. Include corn, black beans, and zucchini noodles in the dish. Cook for five to seven minutes or until the zoodles are tender.
4. Stir in the lime juice, salt, pepper, and Cajun spice until well combined. Add two to three minutes more to the cooking time.
5. You should immediately serve it after garnishing it with fresh cilantro.

129.   SPICY COLLARD GREEN WRAPS

Total Time: 30 minutes

Prep Time: 15 minutes

Ingredients:

- 8 large collard green leaves
- 1 cup quinoa, cooked
- 1 can black beans, drained and rinsed
- 1 cup cherry tomatoes, diced
- 1 avocado, sliced

- 1/2 red onion, finely chopped
- 1/4 cup fresh cilantro, chopped
- 1 lime, juiced
- 2 tablespoons hot sauce
- Salt and pepper to taste

Directions:

1. Collard green leaves should be blanched in water that is boiling for two minutes. Remove, then put to the side to cool off.
2. Take a large bowl and combine the following Ingredients: quinoa, black beans, cherry tomatoes, avocado, red onion, and cilantro.
3. The lime juice, spicy sauce, salt, and pepper should be mixed together in a small bowl using a whisk. Following the pouring, toss the quinoa mixture until it is thoroughly incorporated.
4. The quinoa mixture should be distributed among the collard green leaves that have been laid out. When you roll them up, make sure to tuck the sides in as you go.
5. Each wrap should be cut in half and served as soon as possible. Savor the deliciously spicy flavor!

130.   VEGAN RED BEAN AND KALE SOUP

Total Time: 1 hour

Prep Time: 15 minutes

Ingredients:

- 1 cup red beans, soaked overnight
- 1 tablespoon olive oil
- 1 onion, diced
- 3 cloves garlic, minced
- 2 carrots, peeled and chopped
- 2 celery stalks, chopped
- 1 bunch kale, stems removed and leaves chopped
- 1 can diced tomatoes
- 6 cups vegetable broth
- 1 teaspoon thyme
- 1 teaspoon smoked paprika
- Salt and pepper to taste

Directions:

1. Melt the olive oil in a big saucepan over medium heat.
2. Sauté the onions and garlic until they have become more tender.
3. Carrots, celery, and kale should be added. Cook for five minutes or until the veggies start to become more tender.
4. Be sure to incorporate chopped tomatoes, diced red beans, vegetable broth, smoked paprika, thyme, salt, and pepper into the mixture. Immediately after bringing the water to a boil, immediately decrease the heat to a simmer and continue cooking for forty-five minutes or until the beans are cooked, whichever comes first.
5. To taste, adjust the spice, and serve the dish hot. On a chilly evening, this substantial soup made with red beans and kale is the ideal choice.

131.   VEGAN JAMBALAYA SOUP

Total Time: 45 minutes

Prep Time: 20 minutes

Ingredients:

- 1 cup brown rice, cooked
- 1 tablespoon olive oil
- 1 onion, diced
- 3 bell peppers (red, green, and yellow), diced
- 3 celery stalks, chopped
- 3 cloves garlic, minced
- 1 can diced tomatoes
- 1 cup okra, sliced
- 1 cup vegetable broth
- 1 teaspoon thyme
- 1 teaspoon smoked paprika
- 1/2 teaspoon cayenne pepper
- Salt and pepper to taste

Directions:

1. Melt the olive oil in a big saucepan over medium heat. Include garlic, onions, bell peppers, and celery in the mixture. To ensure that the veggies are cooked through.
2. Rice that has been cooked, diced tomatoes, okra, vegetable broth, thyme, smoked paprika, cayenne pepper, salt, and pepper should be heated together and stirred in. Continue cooking for twenty to twenty-five minutes after bringing the liquid to a simmer point.
3. To taste, adjust the spice, and serve the dish hot. Jambalaya soup is a traditional Cajun dish, but this vegan version is a lovely variation of the cuisine.

132.   VEGAN MARDI GRAS SUSHI

Total Time: 40 minutes

Prep Time: 30 minutes

Ingredients:

- 2 cups sushi rice, cooked
- 1/4 cup rice vinegar
- 1 tablespoon sugar
- 1 teaspoon salt
- 10 nori sheets
- 1 avocado, sliced
- 1 cup shredded purple cabbage
- 1 cup shredded carrots
- 1 cucumber, julienned
- Soy sauce and pickled ginger for serving

Directions:

1. It is recommended that the rice vinegar, sugar, and salt be mixed together in a little basin.
2. Mix this mixture with the sushi rice that has been cooked, and give it a little toss to incorporate.
3. Place a sheet of nori on top of a sushi mat made of bamboo. After spreading a thin layer of sushi rice over the nori, leave a border of one inch at the top of the serving.
4. Along the bottom border of the rice, arrange the avocado, purple cabbage, carrots, and cucumber in a decorative pattern.
5. The sushi should be rolled up securely using the bamboo mat, and the edge should be sealed with a little damp water.
6. Cut the roll into pieces that are the size of bites, and continue the process with the other ingredients.
7. It is recommended that the vegan Mardi Gras sushi be served with pickled ginger and soy sauce. Enjoy this dish that is both festive and bright!

133. CAJUN-STYLE VEGAN CORN FRITTERS

Total Time: 30 minutes

Prep Time: 15 minutes

Ingredients:

- 2 cups fresh or frozen corn kernels
- 1 cup chickpea flour
- 1/4 cup finely chopped green onions
- 1/4 cup chopped red bell pepper
- 1 teaspoon Cajun seasoning
- 1/2 teaspoon baking powder
- Salt and pepper to taste
- Vegetable oil for frying

Directions:

1. Corn kernels, chickpea flour, green onions, red bell pepper, Cajun spice, baking powder, salt, and pepper should be mixed together in a basin before being added to the mixture.
2. Combine well to get a thick batter. In order to reach the desired consistency, you may need to add a small amount of water.
3. The vegetable oil should be brought to a simmer in a skillet that is set over medium heat.
4. Put spoonfuls of the batter into the heated oil and cook them until they are golden brown on all sides by dropping them in.
5. Once the fritters have been removed from the oil, lay them on paper towels so that any leftover oil may drain out.
6. While still hot, serve with the vegan dipping sauce of your choice.

134.　CAJUN CHICKPEA FRITTERS

Total Time: 40 minutes

Prep Time: 20 minutes

Ingredients:

- 2 cans (15 oz each) chickpeas, drained and rinsed
- 1/2 cup breadcrumbs
- 1/4 cup finely chopped celery
- 2 tablespoons Cajun seasoning
- 1 tablespoon ground flaxseed mixed with 3 tablespoons water (flax egg)
- Oil for frying

Directions:

1. Place the chickpeas, breadcrumbs, celery, Cajun spice, and flax egg into a food processor and pulse until smooth.
2. Process the ingredients in a food processor until they come together but have some texture.
3. Shape the ingredients into patties of a smaller size.
4. In a skillet, bring the oil to a setting of medium heat.
5. The chickpea patties should be fried until they are golden brown on all sides.
6. Once the extra oil has been drained on paper towels, serve the dish with a vegan remoulade on the side.

135.   CAJUN CAULIFLOWER WINGS

Total Time: 45 minutes

Prep Time: 20 minutes

Ingredients:

- 1 head cauliflower, cut into florets
- 1 cup flour
- 1 cup plant-based milk
- 2 teaspoons Cajun seasoning
- 1 teaspoon garlic powder
- 1 teaspoon onion powder
- 1/2 teaspoon paprika
- Salt and pepper to taste
- Vegan buffalo sauce for coating

Directions:

1. Set aside a baking sheet and line it with parchment paper once the oven reaches 450 degrees Fahrenheit (230 degrees Celsius).
2. In order to make a batter, combine the following ingredients in a bowl: flour, plant-based milk, Cajun spice, garlic powder, onion powder, paprika, salt, and pepper. Whisk until smooth.
3. It is important to ensure that each cauliflower floret is well covered with the batter before placing it on the baking sheet that has been prepared.
4. The cauliflower should be baked for twenty-five to thirty minutes or until it is golden and crispy.
5. After the cauliflower has been cooked, toss it with vegan buffalo sauce until it is completely covered.
6. Celery sticks and vegan ranch dressing should be served hot with the dish.

136. CREOLE RATATOUILLE

Total Time: 1 hour

Prep Time: 20 minutes

Ingredients:

- 1 eggplant, diced
- 2 zucchini, sliced
- 1 yellow bell pepper, diced
- 1 red onion, chopped
- 3 tomatoes, diced
- 3 cloves garlic, minced

- 2 tablespoons tomato paste
- 1 tablespoon Creole seasoning
- 1 teaspoon dried thyme
- Salt and pepper to taste
- Olive oil

Directions:

1. Bake at a temperature of 190 degrees Celsius (375 degrees Fahrenheit).
2. It is recommended to combine the following ingredients in a big bowl: eggplant, zucchini, bell pepper, red onion, tomatoes, garlic, tomato paste, Creole spice, thyme, salt, and pepper. Combine thoroughly.
3. The vegetable combination should be tossed with olive oil once it has been drizzled over it.
4. Put the mixture in a baking dish and spread it out so that it is equally distributed.
5. Bake for forty to forty-five minutes, tossing the veggies around every so often until they are soft.
6. Whether you want to serve the Creole ratatouille as a side dish or as a whole dinner, serve it over rice.

137.   SMOKY VEGAN RED BEAN HUMMUS

Total Time: 15 minutes

Prep Time: 10 minutes

Ingredients:

- 1 can (15 oz) red beans, drained and rinsed
- 1/4 cup tahini
- 3 tablespoons olive oil
- 2 cloves garlic, minced
- 2 tablespoons lemon juice
- 1 teaspoon smoked paprika
- 1/2 teaspoon cayenne pepper (adjust to taste)
- Salt and pepper to taste
- 2 tablespoons chopped fresh parsley for garnish

Directions:

1. Put the red beans, tahini, olive oil, garlic, lemon juice, smoked paprika, cayenne pepper, salt, and pepper into a food processor. Process until everything is combined.
2. Process until the mixture is silky smooth and creamy, scraping down the sides as necessary.
3. Take a taste, and if required, adjust the spices.
4. Transfer the mixture to a bowl that is suitable for serving, drizzle it with a little olive oil, and top it with chopped parsley.
5. Put on crackers, pita chips, or vegetable sticks of your choice to accompany this dish.

138.   VEGAN GRITS AND MUSHROOM GRAVY

Total Time: 30 minutes

Prep Time: 10 minutes

Ingredients:

- 1 cup grits
- 4 cups vegetable broth
- 1 cup almond milk (unsweetened)
- Salt and pepper to taste
- 2 tablespoons olive oil
- 1 onion, finely chopped
- 2 cloves garlic, minced

- 8 oz mushrooms, sliced
- 1/4 cup all-purpose flour
- 2 cups vegetable broth
- 1 teaspoon thyme
- 1 teaspoon sage
- Chopped green onions for garnish

Directions:

1. Using vegetable broth and almond milk, prepare grits in accordance with the directions provided on the box. Use pepper and salt to season the food.
2. Take a pan and place it over medium heat. Warm the olive oil.
3. Sauté the onions and garlic until they have become more tender.
4. Add the mushrooms to the pan after cooking them until they release their moisture.
5. Add flour to the mushroom mixture, then swirl it to ensure that it is evenly coated. Cook for a total of two minutes.
6. Using a whisk, gradually incorporate the thyme, sage, and vegetable broth. The gravy should be simmered until the right consistency is achieved.
7. The mushroom gravy should be served on top of the cooked grits, and chopped green onions should be used as a garnish.

139.   VEGAN BOUDIN SLIDERS

Total Time: 45 minutes

Prep Time: 20 minutes

Ingredients:

- 1 cup cooked and cooled quinoa
- 1 can (15 oz) black beans, drained and rinsed
- 1 cup breadcrumbs
- 1/2 cup finely chopped onion
- 2 cloves garlic, minced
- 1 teaspoon paprika
- 1 teaspoon Cajun seasoning
- Salt and pepper to taste
- Slider buns
- Lettuce, tomato, and pickles for toppings

Directions:

1. In a food processor, pulse together the quinoa, black beans, breadcrumbs, onion, garlic, paprika, Cajun spice, salt, and pepper until everything is well mixed, pulse.
2. Form the ingredients into patties and cook over medium heat in a skillet until browned all over.
3. The slider buns should be toasted, and then the patties, lettuce, tomato, and pickles should be assembled into sliders.

140.   CAJUN-STYLE VEGAN CAESAR SALAD

Total Time: 20 minutes

Prep Time: 15 minutes

Ingredients:

- 1 head romaine lettuce, chopped
- 1 cup cherry tomatoes, halved
- 1/2 cup croutons
- 1/4 cup vegan Caesar dressing
- 1/4 cup nutritional yeast

- 1 tablespoon capers, drained
- 1 teaspoon Dijon mustard
- Juice of 1 lemon
- 2 cloves garlic, minced
- Salt and pepper to taste

Directions:

1. Put the romaine lettuce, cherry tomatoes, and croutons into a big bowl and mix them together.
2. To make vegan Caesar dressing, combine nutritional yeast, capers, Dijon mustard, lemon juice, garlic, salt, and pepper in a small bowl and mix all of the ingredients together.
3. Once the dressing has been poured over the salad, toss it until it is evenly coated.
4. Immediately serve, and if wanted, garnish with more croutons of your choice.

141. VEGAN BAYOU BISCUITS

Total Time: 30 minutes

Prep Time: 15 minutes

Ingredients:

- 2 cups all-purpose flour
- 1 tablespoon baking powder
- 1/2 teaspoon baking soda
- 1/2 teaspoon salt

- 1 cup unsweetened almond milk
- 1/4 cup vegan butter, melted
- 1 tablespoon apple cider vinegar

Directions:

1. Prior to baking, set the oven temperature to 425 degrees Fahrenheit (220 degrees Celsius).
2. A whisk should be used to combine the components of the cake, which are flour, baking soda, baking powder, and salt. The ingredients should be combined together in a medium-sized basin. In a separate dish, whisk together the almond milk and apple cider vinegar. To allow the curd to solidify, let it sit for five minutes.
3. Pour the vegan butter that has been melted into the combination of almond milk.
4. After adding the liquid components to the dry ones, stir the mixture until it is almost completely incorporated.
5. Scoop the dough out by the spoonful and place it on a parchment-lined baking sheet.
6. For 12 to 15 minutes, or until the tops are a golden brown color, bake the cookies.
7. Warm up your Vegan Bayou Biscuits, and enjoy them to the fullest!

142. VEGAN DIRTY CAULIFLOWER RICE

Total Time: 45 minutes

Prep Time: 15 minutes

Ingredients:

- 1 large cauliflower, grated
- 2 tablespoons vegetable oil
- 1 onion, finely chopped
- 2 bell peppers, diced
- 3 cloves garlic, minced
- 1 cup okra, sliced
- 1 can black beans, drained and rinsed
- 2 teaspoons Cajun seasoning
- Salt and pepper to taste
- Green onions for garnish

Directions:

1. The vegetable oil should be brought to a simmer in a skillet that is set over medium heat.
2. The garlic, onions, and bell peppers should be added. To soften the meat, sauté it.
3. To the mixture, add sliced okra and shredded cauliflower. Bake for ten to twelve minutes, stirring the mixture regularly.
4. The Cajun spice and black beans should be stirred in. Wait an extra five minutes before serving.
5. Before seasoning with salt, add pepper and salt to taste.
6. You may serve your Vegan Dirty Cauliflower Rice while it is still hot and garnish it with chopped green onions.

143.   VEGAN MUFFULETTA PASTA SALAD

Total Time: 30 minutes

Prep Time: 15 minutes

Ingredients:

- 8 oz pasta, cooked and cooled
- 1 cup cherry tomatoes, halved
- 1/2 cup green olives, sliced
- 1/2 cup black olives, sliced
- 1/2 cup artichoke hearts, chopped
- 1/2 cup roasted red peppers, diced
- 1/4 cup red onion, finely chopped
- 1/4 cup fresh parsley, chopped
- 1/2 cup vegan mozzarella, cubed
- 1/4 cup olive oil
- 2 tablespoons red wine vinegar
- 1 teaspoon dried oregano
- Salt and pepper to taste

Directions:

1. All of the following ingredients should be combined in a big bowl: cooked pasta, cherry tomatoes, olives, artichoke hearts, roasted red peppers, red onion, parsley, and vegan mozzarella.
2. Gather all of the ingredients in a small bowl and whisk together the olive oil, red wine vinegar, dried oregano, salt, and pepper.
3. After adding the dressing to the pasta salad, mix it to blend the ingredients.
4. Before serving, place in the refrigerator for at least fifteen minutes.
5. Enjoy the tastes of the Bayou by serving your Vegan Muffuletta Pasta Salad, which should be served cold.

144. CREOLE-STYLE RATATOUILLE

Total Time: 1 hour

Prep Time: 20 minutes

Ingredients:

- 1 eggplant, diced
- 1 zucchini, diced
- 1 yellow squash, diced
- 1 bell pepper, diced
- 1 onion, diced
- 3 cloves garlic, minced
- 1 can diced tomatoes
- 2 tablespoons tomato paste
- 1 teaspoon dried thyme
- 1 teaspoon dried oregano
- 1 teaspoon paprika
- Salt and pepper to taste
- Fresh basil for garnish

Directions:

1. Get the oven hot, about 190 degrees Celsius (375 degrees Fahrenheit).
2. The onion and garlic should be cooked in a large ovenproof pan until they become more pliable.
3. Incorporate bell pepper, zucchini, yellow squash, and eggplant into the dish. 5-7 minutes of cooking time.
4. Add the chopped tomatoes, tomato paste, paprika, oregano, thyme, salt, and pepper. Mix well.
5. Put the pan in the oven and bake it for thirty to thirty-five minutes or until the veggies are cooked, whichever comes first.
6. Add some fresh basil as a garnish before serving your Ratatouille prepared in the Creole style.

145.   GRITS AND GREENS BOWL

Total Time: 30 minutes

Prep Time: 10 minutes

Ingredients:

- 1 cup grits
- 2 cups water
- 1 cup almond milk
- Salt and pepper to taste
- 2 cups kale, chopped
- 1 cup cherry tomatoes, halved
- 1/2 cup red bell pepper, diced
- 1 tablespoon olive oil
- 2 cloves garlic, minced
- 1 tablespoon Cajun seasoning
- 1/4 cup green onions, chopped

Directions:

1. Heat the almond milk and water in a pot until they boil, stirring regularly. Mix in the grits, then cook them in accordance with the directions on the package. Use pepper and salt to season the food.
2. Take a pan and place it over medium heat. Warm the olive oil.
3. Add the garlic, kale, tomatoes, and bell pepper to the mixture. The veggies should be sautéed until they are soft.
4. While continuing to simmer for another two to three minutes, stir in the Cajun spice.
5. After the grits have been cooked, place them in bowls, then top them with veggies that have been sautéed topped with green onions.
6. Make sure to serve your Grits and Greens Bowl while it is still hot.

146. SWEET POTATO AND KALE GUMBO

Total Time: 45 minutes

Prep Time: 15 minutes

Ingredients:

- 2 tablespoons olive oil
- 1 onion, diced
- 2 cloves garlic, minced
- 2 sweet potatoes, peeled and diced
- 1 bell pepper, diced
- 2 cups kale, chopped
- 1 can (15 oz) diced tomatoes
- 4 cups vegetable broth
- 1 cup okra, sliced
- 1 cup cooked red beans
- 1 tablespoon Cajun seasoning
- Salt and pepper to taste
- Cooked rice for serving

Directions:

1. Melt the olive oil in a big saucepan over medium heat.
2. To create a fragrant aroma, sauté the onion and garlic.
3. Include kale, sweet potatoes, and bell peppers in the dish. Maintain a stirring motion every five minutes while cooking.
4. Incorporate chopped tomatoes, okra, red beans, Cajun spice, salt, and pepper into the mixture. Also, use vegetable broth. After bringing to a simmer, cook for 25 to 30 minutes.
5. Serve the spice over rice that has been cooked, and adjust it to taste.
6. Take pleasure in the savory Gumbo made with Sweet Potatoes and Kale!

147.   CREOLE LENTIL AND SPINACH STUFFED MUSHROOMS

Total Time: 40 minutes

Prep Time: 20 minutes

Ingredients:

- 1 cup green lentils, cooked
- 1 cup spinach, chopped
- 1/2 cup breadcrumbs
- 1/4 cup red onion, finely chopped
- 2 cloves garlic, minced
- 1 teaspoon Creole seasoning
- 1/4 cup tomato sauce
- 12 large mushrooms, stems removed
- Olive oil for brushing

Directions:

1. Get the oven hot, about 190 degrees Celsius (375 degrees Fahrenheit).
2. Put the lentils that have been cooked, the spinach, the breadcrumbs, the red onion, the garlic, the Creole spice, and the tomato sauce into a bowl.
3. Once the mushroom caps have been brushed with olive oil, fill them with the lentil mixture.
4. After placing the packed mushrooms on a baking sheet, then bake them for twenty to twenty-five minutes or until they are soft.
5. To serve as an appetizer or a side dish, serve it warm. Savor the Creole Lentil and spinach-stuffed mushrooms that you have prepared.

148. VEGAN CREOLE RATATOUILLE

Total Time: 50 minutes

Prep Time: 15 minutes

Ingredients:

- 1 eggplant, diced
- 1 zucchini, diced
- 1 yellow squash, diced
- 1 bell pepper, diced
- 1 onion, diced
- 3 cloves garlic, minced
- 1 can (15 oz) diced tomatoes

- 2 tablespoons tomato paste
- 1 teaspoon dried thyme
- 1 teaspoon dried oregano
- 1 teaspoon Cajun seasoning
- Salt and pepper to taste
- Fresh basil for garnish

Directions:

1. Get the oven hot, about 190 degrees Celsius (375 degrees Fahrenheit).
2. It is recommended to combine the following ingredients in a big bowl: eggplant, zucchini, yellow squash, bell pepper, onion, and garlic.
3. In a separate dish, combine chopped tomatoes, tomato paste, thyme, oregano, Cajun spice, salt, and pepper. Thoroughly blend until thoroughly combined.
4. To prepare a baking dish, spread a thin layer of the tomato mixture. Spread the vegetable mixture on top of it.
5. Over the veggies, pour the leftover tomato mixture that has been prepared. Bake with the lid on for thirty to thirty-five minutes.
6. Take off the cover and continue baking for another ten to fifteen minutes or until the veggies are soft.
7. Use fresh basil as a garnish, and serve the dish hot. Delight in your Ratatouille made with vegan creole!

149. CAJUN CHICKPEA WRAPS

Total Time: 30 minutes

Prep Time: 15 minutes

Servings: 4

Ingredients:

- 2 cans (15 oz each) chickpeas, drained and rinsed
- 1 tablespoon Cajun seasoning
- 2 tablespoons olive oil
- 4 whole-grain wraps
- 1 cup shredded lettuce
- 1 cup diced tomatoes
- 1/2 cup diced red onion
- 1/4 cup chopped fresh cilantro
- Vegan ranch dressing (optional)

Directions:

1. Chickpeas should be tossed with Cajun spice in a basin until they are completely covered.
2. Set the olive oil over medium heat in a skillet.
3. Sauté the chickpeas until they get crispy, which should take around eight to ten minutes.
4. You may reheat the wraps in the microwave or in a dry skillet.
5. Putting together wraps involves layering chickpeas, lettuce, tomatoes, red onion, and cilantro in a certain order.
6. Depending on your preference, drizzle with vegan ranch dressing.
7. Close the roll securely and serve it right away.

150. CAJUN CORN CHOWDER

Total Time: 45 minutes

Prep Time: 15 minutes

Servings: 6

Ingredients:

- 4 cups fresh or frozen corn kernels
- 1 onion, diced
- 2 potatoes, peeled and diced
- 3 cloves garlic, minced
- 1 tablespoon Cajun seasoning
- 4 cups vegetable broth
- 1 cup unsweetened almond milk
- Salt and pepper to taste
- Green onions, chopped (for garnish)

Directions:

1. Sauté the onion and garlic in a large saucepan until they have become more pliable.
2. Add the Cajun spice, potatoes, and corn to the dish. Cook for a period of five minutes.
3. After adding the vegetable broth, bring the mixture to a boil. The potatoes should be cooked at a low simmer until they are soft.
4. Take a portion of the soup and puree it with an immersion blender, but be sure to leave some lumps for texture.
5. After incorporating the almond milk, season it with salt and pepper.
6. For a further ten minutes, continue to simmer. Green onions should be used as a garnish before serving.

151.   DIRTY RICE STUFFED ZUCCHINI

Total Time: 1 hour

Prep Time: 20 minutes

Servings: 8

Ingredients:

- 4 large zucchinis, halved lengthwise
- 1 cup brown rice, cooked
- 1 onion, finely diced
- 1 bell pepper, diced
- 2 celery stalks, diced
- 3 cloves garlic, minced
- 1 cup black beans, cooked
- 1 tablespoon Cajun seasoning
- 1/4 cup tomato sauce
- 2 tablespoons olive oil
- Salt and pepper to taste

Directions:

1. Get the oven hot, about 190 degrees Celsius (375 degrees Fahrenheit).
2. Using a spoon, remove the heart of the zucchinis, leaving behind the shell. Scoop out the zucchini and chop it.
3. Get the olive oil going in a skillet and sauté the garlic, onion, bell pepper, and celery until they're soft.
4. Cajun spice, black beans, and freshly cut zucchini should be added. Cook for a period of five minutes.
5. Tomato sauce and cooked rice should be stirred in. Use pepper and salt to season the food.
6. The rice mixture should be stuffed into the halves of the zucchini.
7. Put the zucchini in a baking dish and bake them for thirty to thirty-five minutes or until they are soft.

152. SPICY VEGAN JAMBALAYA

Total Time: 50 minutes

Prep Time: 15 minutes

Servings: 6

Ingredients:

- 1 cup brown rice, uncooked
- 1 onion, diced
- 1 bell pepper, diced
- 2 celery stalks, diced
- 3 cloves garlic, minced
- 1 can (14 oz) diced tomatoes
- 1 cup okra, sliced
- 1 cup vegetable broth
- 1 tablespoon Cajun seasoning
- 1 teaspoon smoked paprika
- 1 cup kidney beans, cooked
- Salt and pepper to taste
- Fresh parsley, chopped (for garnish)

Directions:

1. Cook the brown rice in accordance with the directions on the box.
2. Sauté the onion, bell pepper, celery, and garlic in a large saucepan until the vegetables have become more tender.
3. Incorporate chopped tomatoes, okra, smoked paprika, Cajun spice, and vegetable broth into the mixture. Allow coming to a simmer.
4. Mix in kidney beans and rice that has been cooked. Add another ten to fifteen minutes of cooking time.
5. Before seasoning with salt, add pepper and salt to taste.
6. Immediately prior to serving, garnish with fresh parsley.

153. CREOLE CABBAGE ROLLS

Total Time: 1 hour 30 minutes

Prep Time: 30 minutes

Servings: 4

Ingredients:

- 1 large cabbage head
- 1 cup quinoa, cooked
- 1 can (15 oz) black beans, drained and rinsed
- 1 cup corn kernels (fresh or frozen)
- 1 bell pepper, finely diced
- 1 onion, finely diced
- 3 cloves garlic, minced
- 1 teaspoon Cajun seasoning
- 1 can (15 oz) tomato sauce
- Salt and pepper to taste
- Chopped fresh parsley for garnish

Directions:

1. While baking, bring to 190 degrees Celsius (375 degrees Fahrenheit).
2. Bring the water in a big saucepan to a boil. Add the entire cabbage and continue to boil for another five to seven minutes or until the leaves become flexible. Then, remove it, drain it, and allow it to cool.
3. Mix together the quinoa, black beans, corn, bell pepper, onion, garlic, Cajun spice, salt, and pepper in a large mixing bowl. Blend until everything is well distributed.
4. Take the cabbage leaves and carefully peel them off. Then, spoon a dollop of the quinoa mixture inside of each cabbage leaf. Press the seam side down and roll the dough tightly before placing it in a baking tray.
5. Make sure that the cabbage rolls are uniformly covered with tomato sauce by pouring it over them.
6. To ensure that the cabbage is soft, bake it for thirty to forty minutes.
7. The dish should be served hot and garnished with minced parsley.

154. CREOLE-STYLE STUFFED ZUCCHINI BOATS

Total Time: 45 minutes

Prep Time: 15 minutes

Servings: 3-4

Ingredients:

- 3 large zucchinis, halved lengthwise
- 1 cup cooked brown rice
- 1 can (14 oz) diced tomatoes, drained
- 1 cup black-eyed peas, cooked
- 1 bell pepper, diced
- 1 celery stalk, diced
- 1 onion, finely chopped
- 2 cloves garlic, minced
- 1 teaspoon Cajun seasoning
- 1 tablespoon tomato paste
- Salt and pepper to taste
- Chopped green onions for garnish

Directions:

1. Get the oven hot, about 190 degrees Celsius (375 degrees Fahrenheit).
2. Take the zucchinis and scoop out the center to make boats, leaving a border of approximately half an inch around the zucchinis.
3. Rice, diced tomatoes, black-eyed peas, bell pepper, celery, onion, garlic, Cajun spice, tomato paste, salt, and pepper should be combined in a bowl and then stirred together.
4. Place a little of the mixture inside of each zucchini boat.
5. After filling, place the zucchini on a baking tray and tender it with foil.
6. Until the zucchinis are soft, bake them for twenty-five to thirty minutes.
7. Include some chopped green onions as a garnish, and then serve.

155.　CREOLE QUINOA SALAD

Total Time: 20 minutes

Prep Time: 10 minutes

Servings: 4

Ingredients:

- 2 cups cooked quinoa, cooled
- 1 can (15 oz) black beans, drained and rinsed
- 1 cup cherry tomatoes, halved
- 1 cucumber, diced
- 1 bell pepper, diced
- 1/4 cup red onion, finely chopped
- 1/4 cup fresh parsley, chopped
- 2 tablespoons olive oil
- 1 tablespoon apple cider vinegar
- 1 teaspoon Cajun seasoning
- Salt and pepper to taste
- Lemon wedges for serving

Directions:

1. Put the quinoa, black beans, cherry tomatoes, cucumber, bell pepper, red onion, and parsley into a big bowl and mix them together before serving.
2. Olive oil, apple cider vinegar, Cajun spice, salt, and pepper should be mixed together in a small bowl after being whisked together.
3. After the dressing has been poured over the quinoa mixture, toss it until it is thoroughly incorporated.
4. Prepare and serve cold, with slices of lemon on the side.

156. DIRTY RICE STUFFED TOMATOES

Total Time: 50 minutes

Prep Time: 20 minutes

Servings: 6

Ingredients:

- 6 large tomatoes, tops removed and insides scooped out
- 1 cup brown rice, cooked
- 1 cup vegan sausage, crumbled
- 1 onion, finely diced
- 1 bell pepper, finely diced
- 3 celery stalks, finely diced
- 2 cloves garlic, minced
- 1 teaspoon Cajun seasoning
- 1/2 cup vegetable broth
- Salt and pepper to taste
- Chopped green onions for garnish

Directions:

1. Get the oven hot, about 190 degrees Celsius (375 degrees Fahrenheit).
2. Cook the vegan sausage in a pan until it has a browned appearance. Take out and put to the side.
3. Sauté the onion, bell pepper, celery, and garlic in the same pan until the vegetables have become more tender.
4. Rice that has been cooked, vegan sausage, Cajun spice, vegetable broth, salt, and pepper should be stirred in by hand.
5. Place each tomato on a baking dish after stuffing it with the rice mixture and placing it in the oven.
6. Until the tomatoes are soft, bake them for twenty-five to thirty minutes.
7. Include some chopped green onions as a garnish, and then serve.

157. VEGAN DIRTY QUINOA

Total Time: 30 minutes

Prep Time: 10 minutes

Ingredients:

- 1 cup quinoa, rinsed
- 2 cups vegetable broth
- 1 tablespoon olive oil
- 1 onion, diced
- 3 cloves garlic, minced
- 1 bell pepper, diced
- 1 celery stalk, chopped
- 1 can (15 oz) black beans, drained and rinsed
- 1 teaspoon Cajun seasoning
- Salt and pepper to taste
- Green onions for garnish

Directions:

1. Quinoa and vegetable broth should be mixed together in a medium-sized pot. After bringing it to a boil, decrease the heat to low, cover it, and continue to simmer for fifteen to twenty minutes or until the quinoa is cooked.
2. In a large pan, begin by heating the olive oil over medium heat.
3. Include celery, onion, garlic, and bell pepper in the mixture. To ensure that the veggies are cooked through.
4. Cajun seasoning, black beans, quinoa that has been cooked, and salt and pepper should be stirred in. To let the flavors combine, continue cooking for an additional five minutes.
5. The dish should be served warm and garnished with chopped green onions.

158. BLACKENED TEMPEH PO' BOY

Total Time: 40 minutes

Prep Time: 15 minutes

Ingredients:

- 1 package (8 oz) tempeh, sliced
- 2 tablespoons Cajun seasoning
- 2 tablespoons olive oil
- 4 French bread rolls

- Vegan mayo
- Shredded lettuce
- Sliced tomatoes
- Pickles

Directions:

1. Season the tempeh slices with Cajun spice and rub it into both sides.
2. While the olive oil is boiling, lower the heat to medium-high. After cooking for three to four minutes on each side, tempeh should be blackened.
3. Spread vegan mayonnaise on each side of the French bread rolls that you have sliced.
4. The rolls should be topped with shredded lettuce, sliced tomatoes, and pickles, and then the tempeh should be rolled up and blackened.
5. Immediately serve and savor the deliciousness of your Blackened Tempeh Po'Boy!

159.   VEGAN CRAWFISH PASTA

Total Time: 45 minutes

Prep Time: 20 minutes

Ingredients:

- 8 oz linguine or your favorite pasta
- 1 tablespoon olive oil
- 1 onion, finely chopped
- 2 cloves garlic, minced
- 1 bell pepper, diced
- 1 cup vegan crawfish (or hearts of palm)

- 1 can (14 oz) diced tomatoes
- 1 teaspoon Cajun seasoning
- 1/2 cup vegetable broth
- Salt and pepper to taste
- Fresh parsley for garnish

Directions:

1. Pasta should be cooked according to package recommendations. After draining, save aside for future use.
2. In a large pan, begin by heating the olive oil over medium heat. Sauté the garlic, onion, and bell pepper in a small skillet. To soften the meat, sauté it.
3. The addition of chopped tomatoes, vegan crawfish, Cajun spice, and veggie broth is recommended. Warm for fifteen to twenty minutes.
4. Before seasoning with salt, add pepper and salt to taste. Add the cooked spaghetti and toss it until it is completely incorporated.
5. Add some fresh parsley as a garnish, and serve your vegan crab pasta while it is still hot.

160.   VEGAN MIRLITON AND BLACK BEAN TACOS

Total Time: 35 minutes

Prep Time: 15 minutes

Ingredients:

- 2 mirlitons (chayotes), peeled and diced
- 1 can (15 oz) black beans, drained and rinsed
- 1 tablespoon olive oil
- 1 onion, diced
- 2 cloves garlic, minced
- 1 teaspoon Cajun seasoning
- Corn tortillas
- Avocado slices
- Lime wedges
- Fresh cilantro for garnish

Directions:

1. In salted water, bring chopped mirliton to a boil until it is soft. Drain, then keep away for later use.
2. In a pan over medium heat, warm the olive oil to prepare it.
3. Include the garlic and onion. Sauté till the aroma rises.
4. Incorporate mirliton that has been cooked, black beans, and Cajun spice. Add another five to seven minutes of cooking time.
5. Corn tortillas should be warmed before being filled with the combination of mirliton and black beans.
6. A squeeze of lime, slices of avocado, and fresh cilantro are the garnishes that should be placed on top. Bring your Vegan Tacos with Mirliton and Black Beans to a warm temperature.

161. BLACKENED TOFU CAESAR WRAP

Total Time: 30 minutes

Prep Time: 15 minutes

Ingredients:

- 1 block extra-firm tofu, pressed and sliced
- 2 tablespoons Cajun seasoning
- 1 tablespoon olive oil
- 4 large whole wheat or spinach tortillas
- 1 cup cherry tomatoes, halved
- 1 cup shredded romaine lettuce
- 1/2 cup vegan Caesar dressing
- Salt and pepper, to taste

Directions:

1. Bring a skillet up to temperature over medium-high heat.
2. Take each slice of tofu and rub the Cajun spice onto both sides of the slice.
3. The tofu should be cooked in the skillet with olive oil for three to four minutes on each side until it becomes browned.
4. You may reheat tortillas in the microwave or in a dry pan.
5. Gather the ingredients for the wraps by stuffing each tortilla with pieces of tofu, tomatoes, and lettuce.
6. Wrap the dish firmly, then drizzle it with Caesar dressing, season it with salt and pepper, and serve.

162.   VEGAN BISCUITS AND CREOLE GRAVY

Total Time: 45 minutes

Prep Time: 15 minutes

Ingredients:

- For Biscuits:
- 2 cups all-purpose flour
- 1 tablespoon baking powder
- 1/2 teaspoon salt
- 1 cup non-dairy milk
- 1/3 cup coconut oil, melted

- For Creole Gravy:
- 2 tablespoons vegan butter
- 2 tablespoons all-purpose flour
- 1 cup vegetable broth
- 1 teaspoon Cajun seasoning
- Salt and pepper, to taste

Directions:

1. To make biscuits, preheat the oven to 425 degrees Fahrenheit (220 degrees Celsius).
2. Coat the flour, baking soda, and salt in equal parts and set aside.
3. Stir until the ingredients are just blended. Add the non-dairy milk and the melted coconut oil.
4. After placing spoonfuls on a baking sheet, bake for 12 to 15 minutes or until the mixture is golden brown.
5. It is necessary to melt vegan butter in a skillet over medium heat in order to make creole gravy.
6. Thoroughly incorporate the flour by mixing it in.
7. Slowly whisk in the vegetable stock so lumps don't form.
8. Add some salt, pepper, and Cajun flavor to the dish. To thicken, continue to simmer.
9. The Creole gravy should be served on top of the biscuits.

163.   CAJUN JACKFRUIT TACOS

Total Time: 35 minutes

Prep Time: 15 minutes

Ingredients:

- 2 cans of young green jackfruit, drained and shredded
- 2 tablespoons Cajun seasoning
- 1 tablespoon olive oil
- 8 small corn tortillas
- 1 cup shredded purple cabbage
- 1 avocado, sliced
- Fresh cilantro for garnish
- Lime wedges for serving

Directions:

1. A saucepan filled with olive oil should be heated to a simmer over medium heat.
2. Sauté the shredded jackfruit and Cajun seasoning for eight to ten minutes after adding them.
3. You may reheat tortillas in the microwave or in a dry pan.
4. Prepare tacos by combining jackfruit, shredded cabbage, avocado slices, and cilantro in a single layer.
5. Lime wedges should be served on the side.

164.   CREOLE-STYLE VEGAN RED LENTIL SOUP

Total Time: 40 minutes

Prep Time: 10 minutes

Ingredients:

- 1 cup red lentils, rinsed
- 1 onion, diced
- 2 celery stalks, chopped
- 2 carrots, diced
- 3 cloves garlic, minced
- 1 can (14 oz) diced tomatoes

- 1 teaspoon Cajun seasoning
- 1 teaspoon dried thyme
- 6 cups vegetable broth
- Salt and pepper, to taste
- Fresh parsley for garnish

Directions:

1. The onions, celery, and carrots should be sautéed in a big saucepan until they become tender.
2. Garlic, Cajun spice, and thyme should be added and cooked for one to two minutes.
3. Incorporate chopped tomatoes, red lentils, and vegetable broth into the mixture.
4. Raise the heat to high, then reduce it to low and simmer for 20–25 minutes or until the lentils are tender.
5. Add some salt and pepper, and before serving, sprinkle some fresh parsley on top as a garnish.

165. RED PEPPER AND ARTICHOKE JAMBALAYA

Total Time: 45 minutes

Prep Time: 15 minutes

Ingredients:

- 2 cups long-grain white rice
- 1 large red bell pepper, diced
- 1 can artichoke hearts, drained and quartered
- 1 onion, finely chopped
- 3 cloves garlic, minced
- 1 can diced tomatoes
- 1 cup vegetable broth
- 1 teaspoon paprika
- 1 teaspoon thyme
- 1 teaspoon oregano
- 1/2 teaspoon cayenne pepper
- Salt and pepper to taste
- 2 tablespoons olive oil
- Fresh parsley for garnish

Directions:

1. Prepare the rice in accordance with the directions on the package.
2. In a pan over medium heat, warm the olive oil to prepare it. Sauté the onions and bell pepper till they have become more tender.
3. Cook for a further one to two minutes after adding the minced garlic until the aroma is released.
4. Combine chopped tomatoes, artichoke hearts, vegetable broth, paprika, thyme, oregano, cayenne pepper, salt, and pepper. Stir until everything is evenly distributed. Allow coming to a simmer.
5. Allow it to boil for twenty to twenty-five minutes until the flavors have merged.
6. Jambalaya should be served over cooked rice, and fresh parsley should be used as a garnish.

166. VEGAN BISCUITS AND GRAVY CAJUN-STYLE

Total Time: 30 minutes

Prep Time: 10 minutes

Ingredients:

- 2 cups all-purpose flour
- 1 tablespoon baking powder
- 1/2 teaspoon salt
- 1 cup unsweetened almond milk
- 1/4 cup vegan butter
- 1/4 cup all-purpose flour (for the gravy)

- 2 cups unsweetened almond milk (for the gravy)
- Salt and pepper to taste
- 1 teaspoon Cajun seasoning
- Vegan sausage crumbles (optional for added texture)

Directions:

1. For optimal results, set your oven temperature to 450 °F or 230 °C.
2. Coat the flour, baking soda, and salt in equal parts and set aside. Incorporate the almond milk gradually while whisking the mixture.
3. To bake the dough, scoop it out onto a baking sheet. Ten to twelve minutes in the oven should be enough time for a golden brown top.
4. Vegan butter should be melted in a pot. In order to make a roux, stir in a quarter cup of flour.
5. Add the almond milk in a slow and steady stream while whisking. Cajun spice, salt, and pepper should be added. Cook until the mixture becomes thick.
6. If you so wish, you may incorporate crumbled vegan sausage.
7. Serve the biscuits with a gravy prepared in the Cajun way on top.

167. VEGAN CRAWFISH ETOUFFEE

Total Time: 1 hour

Prep Time: 20 minutes

Ingredients:

- 1 cup vegan butter
- 1 cup all-purpose flour
- 1 onion, finely chopped
- 1 bell pepper, diced
- 3 celery stalks, diced
- 4 cloves garlic, minced
- 1 can hearts of palm, sliced into chunks (to mimic crawfish)

- 1 cup vegetable broth
- 1 can diced tomatoes
- 2 teaspoons Cajun seasoning
- 1 teaspoon thyme
- Salt and pepper to taste
- Cooked rice for serving

Directions:

1. After melting vegan butter in a big saucepan, whisk in flour until it reaches a golden brown color. This will create a roux.
2. Make sure to include garlic, onions, bell peppers, and celery. To ensure that the veggies are cooked through.
3. Mix in the chopped tomatoes, hearts of palm, vegetable broth, Cajun spice, thyme, salt, and pepper. Hearts of palm are also included.
4. Simmer for thirty to forty minutes, stirring the mixture in between.
5. While the rice is cooking, serve.

168. VEGAN MUFFULETTA PIZZA

Total Time: 25 minutes

Prep Time: 10 minutes

Ingredients:

- 1 pizza dough (store-bought or homemade)
- 1/2 cup vegan olive tapenade
- 1 cup vegan mozzarella, shredded
- 1/2 cup marinated artichoke hearts, chopped
- 1/4 cup sliced black olives
- 1/4 cup sliced green olives
- 1/4 cup roasted red peppers, sliced
- 1/4 cup banana peppers, sliced
- 1 tablespoon capers
- Fresh basil for garnish

Directions:

1. In accordance with the directions provided for the pizza dough, preheat the oven.
2. Using a surface that has been dusted with flour, roll out the pizza dough and then move it to a pizza stone or baking sheet.
3. Olive tapenade should be spread over the dough to serve as the sauce.
4. To finish, sprinkle vegan mozzarella over the tapenade in a uniform layer.
5. Served with capers, artichoke hearts, roasted red peppers, green olives, and green olives, as well as roasted red peppers and banana peppers.
6. Melt the cheese and bake the crust according to the pizza dough package directions until the crust is golden brown.
7. Fresh basil should be used as a garnish before serving.

169. CAJUN RED BEANS AND QUINOA

Total Time: 40 minutes

Prep Time: 10 minutes

Ingredients:

- 1 cup quinoa, rinsed
- 2 cups cooked red beans
- 1 onion, finely chopped
- 1 bell pepper, diced
- 3 cloves garlic, minced
- 2 tablespoons Cajun seasoning

- 1 teaspoon smoked paprika
- 1 can (14 oz) diced tomatoes
- 2 cups vegetable broth
- Salt and pepper to taste
- Green onions for garnish

Directions:

1. Sauté the onion and bell pepper in a saucepan until they have become more tender.
2. Include smoked paprika, garlic, and Cajun seasoning in the mixture. For one to two minutes, cook.
3. Quinoa, red beans, chopped tomatoes, and vegetable broth should be stirred in at this point.
4. The water should be brought to a boil, then lowered to a simmer, and covered for twenty to twenty-five minutes or until the quinoa is done.
5. Use pepper and salt to season the food. Green onions should be used as a garnish before serving.

170.   RED PEPPER GRITS CAKES

Total Time: 45 minutes

Prep Time: 15 minutes

Ingredients:

- 1 cup grits
- 4 cups vegetable broth
- 1 cup red bell pepper, finely chopped
- 1/2 cup green onions, thinly sliced
- 1/2 cup nutritional yeast
- 1 teaspoon Cajun seasoning
- Salt and pepper to taste
- 2 tablespoons olive oil

Directions:

1. Prepare grits in a vegetable broth in accordance with the directions provided on the box.
2. Before serving, garnish with nutritional yeast, Cajun seasoning, chopped green onions, red bell pepper, and salt and pepper. Combine by stirring.
3. Patties should be formed once the liquid has been allowed to slightly cool down.
4. Get the olive oil heated up to medium-high in a skillet.
5. To get a golden brown color on all sides, cook the patties.
6. When served hot, the Cajun-inspired grits cakes are sure to be enjoyed.

171. CAJUN CHICKPEA LETTUCE CUP WRAPS

Total Time: 20 minutes

Prep Time: 15 minutes

Ingredients:

- 1 can (15 oz) chickpeas, drained and rinsed
- 1 tablespoon Cajun seasoning
- 1 tablespoon olive oil
- 1 cup cherry tomatoes, halved
- 1/2 cup red onion, finely diced
- 1/4 cup fresh cilantro, chopped
- Juice of 1 lime
- Salt and pepper to taste
- Lettuce leaves for wrapping

Directions:

1. To prepare the chickpeas, combine them with olive oil and Cajun spice in a dish.
2. Roast the chickpeas for 15 minutes at 400 °F or 200 °C.; then, let them cool.
3. Put the chickpeas that have been roasted along with the tomatoes, red onion, cilantro, lime juice, salt, and pepper.
4. Wraps may be made by taking the mixture and spooning it into lettuce leaves.
5. Serve the tasty Cajun chickpea wraps as soon as possible and relish their deliciousness.

172.   VEGAN CAJUN TOFU SCRAMBLE

Total Time: 25 minutes

Prep Time: 10 minutes

Ingredients:

- 1 block extra-firm tofu, pressed and crumbled
- 1 tablespoon olive oil
- 1 small onion, finely chopped
- 1 bell pepper, diced
- 2 cloves garlic, minced
- 1 teaspoon Cajun seasoning
- 1/2 teaspoon smoked paprika
- 1/4 teaspoon cayenne pepper (adjust to taste)
- Salt and pepper to taste
- 2 green onions, sliced (for garnish)
- Fresh parsley, chopped (for garnish)

Directions:

1. A saucepan filled with olive oil should be heated to a simmer over medium heat.
2. Proceed to sauté the chopped onion until it becomes transparent.
3. Coat the skillet with the minced garlic and diced bell pepper by stirring them together. Please continue to cook for a further two to three minutes until the veggies are soft.
4. Crush the pressed tofu and add it to the skillet, being sure to thoroughly combine it with the veggies.
5. The tofu mixture should be seasoned with Cajun spice, smoked paprika, cayenne pepper, salt, and pepper according to personal preference. Mix everything together so that the spices are distributed evenly.
6. Proceed to cook the tofu for a further eight to ten minutes, tossing it regularly until it reaches a golden color with a small crunch.
7. If necessary, taste the dish and make any necessary adjustments to the spices. You can increase the amount of cayenne pepper if you prefer it spicy.
8. Slice some green onions and sprinkle some garden-fresh parsley on top before serving.
9. If you want to make a dinner that is both tasty and satisfying, serve the Vegan Cajun Tofu Scramble on its own or with bread.

173. VEGAN JAMBALAYA SPRING ROLLS

Total Time: 1 hour

Prep Time: 30 minutes

Yields: 12 spring rolls

Ingredients:

- 1 cup cooked jasmine rice
- 1 cup diced vegan sausage
- 1 cup diced bell peppers (red, green, and yellow)
- 1 cup diced tomatoes
- 1 cup diced okra
- 1 tablespoon Cajun seasoning
- 12 rice paper wrappers
- 1/4 cup chopped fresh cilantro
- 1/4 cup soy sauce (for dipping)

Directions:

1. Rice that has been cooked, vegan sausage, bell peppers, tomatoes, okra, and Cajun spice should be combined in a big bowl.
2. Please prepare the rice paper wrappers in accordance with the directions provided on the box.
3. Take a tablespoon of the rice mixture and place it on each wrapper. Next, add some cilantro and roll the wrappers firmly while tucking in the edges.
4. Include a soy sauce dipping sauce for serving.

174. VEGAN GUMBO POT PIE

Total Time: 1 hour 30 minutes

Prep Time: 45 minutes

Baking Time: 45 minutes

Yields: 6 servings

Ingredients:

- 1 cup chopped okra
- 1 cup diced celery
- 1 cup diced bell peppers (any color)
- 1 cup diced onion
- 1 cup sliced vegan sausage
- 1/2 cup all-purpose flour
- 1/2 cup vegetable oil
- 4 cups vegetable broth
- 1 teaspoon Cajun seasoning
- Salt and pepper to taste
- 1 sheet vegan puff pastry

Directions:

1. Get the oven hot, about 190 degrees Celsius (375 degrees Fahrenheit).
2. Vegetable oil should be used to sauté okra, celery, bell peppers, onion, and vegan sausage in a large saucepan until the veggies are soft.
3. Cook for five minutes after stirring in the flour.
4. Make sure to stir slowly while adding the veggie broth. Add some salt, pepper, and Cajun flavor to the dish. To thicken, continue to simmer.
5. The mixture of gumbo should be poured into a baking dish.
6. The puff pastry should be rolled out and then placed on top of the gumbo mixture. The borders should be sealed.
7. Bake the crust until it reaches a golden brown color.
8. Be sure to give it some time to cool down before serving.

175. CREOLE-STYLE RATATOUILLE PIZZA

Total Time: 45 minutes

Prep Time: 20 minutes

Baking Time: 25 minutes

Yields: 8 slices

Ingredients:

- 1 pre-made pizza crust (vegan)
- 1 cup tomato sauce
- 1 zucchini, thinly sliced
- 1 yellow squash, thinly sliced
- 1 eggplant, thinly sliced
- 1 bell pepper, thinly sliced
- 1 cup cherry tomatoes, halved
- 2 cloves garlic, minced
- 1 teaspoon Creole seasoning
- 1 cup vegan mozzarella cheese
- Fresh basil leaves for garnish

Directions:

1. In accordance with the directions provided for the pizza crust, preheat the oven.
2. Tomato sauce should be spread on top of the pizza dough.
3. To finish, arrange the following vegetables on top: zucchini, yellow squash, eggplant, bell pepper, and cherry tomatoes.
4. Garlic that has been minced and Creole spice should be sprinkled over the veggies.
5. Sprinkle some vegan mozzarella cheese on top.
6. In order to get a golden brown crust and melted, bubbling cheese, bake the dish.
7. Prior to serving, garnish with fresh basil leaves from the garden.

176. CREOLE STUFFED BELL PEPPER CASSEROLE

Total Time: 1 hour

Prep Time: 30 minutes

Baking Time: 30 minutes

Yields: 4 servings

Ingredients:

- 4 large bell peppers, halved and seeds removed
- 1 cup cooked quinoa
- 1 cup black beans, drained and rinsed
- 1 cup corn kernels
- 1 cup diced tomatoes
- 1 cup diced red onion
- 1 teaspoon Creole seasoning
- 1/2 cup vegan shredded cheese
- Fresh parsley for garnish

Directions:

1. Get the oven hot, about 190 degrees Celsius (375 degrees Fahrenheit).
2. Quinoa, black beans, corn, tomatoes, red onion, and Creole spice should be combined in a basin and stirred together.
3. The halves of the bell pepper should be placed in a baking dish.
4. Place a little of the quinoa mixture inside of each pepper half.
5. Top with shredded vegan cheese that has been veganized.
6. After that, bake it for twenty minutes with the foil cover. After 10 more minutes of baking, take the foil off and continue to bake until the peppers are cooked and the cheese has melted.
7. Immediately prior to serving, garnish with fresh parsley.

177.   CAJUN EGGPLANT AND TOMATO SAUTE

Total Time: 30 minutes

Prep Time: 10 minutes

Ingredients:

- 2 large eggplants, diced
- 1 cup cherry tomatoes, halved
- 1 onion, finely chopped
- 3 cloves garlic, minced
- 2 tablespoons Cajun seasoning
- 2 tablespoons olive oil
- Salt and pepper to taste
- Fresh parsley for garnish

Directions:

1. A saucepan filled with olive oil should be heated to a simmer over medium heat.
2. Sauté the onions and garlic until they have become more tender.
3. Add cherry tomatoes and diced eggplants to the pan and stir to combine.
4. On top of the veggies, sprinkle some Cajun spice, along with some salt and pepper.
5. Carefully stir the eggplants and continue cooking them until they are soft but not mushy.
6. While it's still hot, sprinkle chopped fresh parsley on top.

178.   DIRTY RICE STUFFED BELL PEPPERS

Total Time: 1 hour

Prep Time: 20 minutes

Ingredients:

- 4 bell peppers, halved and seeds removed
- 1 cup brown rice, cooked
- 1 cup vegan ground sausage
- 1 onion, finely diced
- 1 celery stalk, finely chopped
- 1 bell pepper, finely chopped
- 2 cloves garlic, minced
- 2 tablespoons Cajun seasoning
- 1 can (15 oz) black beans, drained and rinsed
- 1 cup vegetable broth
- Green onions for garnish

Directions:

1. Get the oven hot, about 190 degrees Celsius (375 degrees Fahrenheit).
2. Sauté the onion, celery, bell pepper, and garlic in a pan until the vegetables have become more tender.
3. Cook the vegan sausage until it has a browned appearance.
4. Rice that has been cooked, black beans, Cajun spice, and vegetable broth should be stirred in.
5. Place the dirty rice mixture inside the bell peppers that have been cut in half.
6. Bake the peppers for thirty to forty minutes, or until they reach the desired level of tenderness, after placing them on a baking dish.
7. Prior to serving, garnish with green onions that have been chopped.

179.   VEGAN BANANA FOSTER SMOOTHIE

Total Time: 10 minutes

Prep Time: 5 minutes

Ingredients:

- 2 ripe bananas
- 1 cup almond milk
- 1 tablespoon maple syrup
- 1 teaspoon vanilla extract
- 1/2 teaspoon ground cinnamon
- 1/4 teaspoon nutmeg
- Ice cubes (optional)
- Sliced bananas for garnish

Directions:

1. Using a blender, add ripe bananas, almond milk, maple syrup, vanilla essence, cinnamon, and nutmeg. Blend until smooth, then serve.
2. Puree till it is silky, smooth, and creamy.
3. If desired, add ice cubes and mix one more until everything is well incorporated.
4. To garnish, pour the mixture into glasses and top with sliced bananas.
5. Serve as soon as possible.

180.   CAJUN CORN AND AVOCADO SALSA

Total Time: 20 minutes

Prep Time: 10 minutes

Ingredients:

- 2 cups fresh or frozen corn kernels
- 1 ripe avocado, diced
- 1 cup cherry tomatoes, halved
- 1/2 red onion, finely chopped
- 1/4 cup fresh cilantro, chopped
- 1 jalapeño, seeded and finely diced
- 2 tablespoons lime juice
- 2 tablespoons olive oil
- 1 teaspoon Cajun seasoning
- Salt and pepper to taste

Directions:

1. The corn, chopped avocado, cherry tomatoes, red onion, cilantro, and jalapeño should be mixed together in a large bowl.
2. Lime juice, olive oil, and Cajun seasoning should be mixed together in a small bowl after being whisked together.
3. The corn and avocado combination should be tossed lightly to blend once the dressing has been poured over it.
4. Before seasoning with salt, add pepper and salt to taste.
5. Leaving the salsa out for a few minutes will allow the flavors to combine and become more pronounced.
6. In addition to serving the Cajun Corn and Avocado Salsa with tortilla chips, you can also use it as a topping for vegan tacos or grilled tofu.

181. CAJUN LENTIL TACOS

Total Time: 40 minutes

Prep Time: 15 minutes

Ingredients:

- 1 cup dried green lentils
- 2 cups vegetable broth
- 1 tablespoon Cajun seasoning
- 1 teaspoon smoked paprika
- 1 teaspoon garlic powder
- 1 tablespoon olive oil

- 8 small taco shells
- 1 cup shredded lettuce
- 1 cup diced tomatoes
- 1/2 cup diced red onions
- 1/2 cup chopped fresh cilantro
- Lime wedges for serving

Directions:

1. Lentils should be washed and then combined with vegetable broth in a saucepan. The lentils should be cooked after about 25 minutes of simmering after the pot has been brought to a boil.
2. Cajun spice, smoked paprika, and garlic powder should be stirred into the lentils after any extra moisture has been drained from them.
3. Warm the olive oil in a separate skillet, then sauté the lentils that have been seasoned for five minutes.
4. In accordance with the instructions on the box, warm taco shells.
5. When putting together tacos, use lentils, lettuce, tomatoes, red onions, and cilantro as the ingredients. Please serve with slices of lime.

182.   CAJUN CHICKPEA FAJITAS

Total Time: 30 minutes

Prep Time: 10 minutes

Ingredients:

- 2 cans (15 oz each) chickpeas, drained and rinsed
- 2 bell peppers, thinly sliced
- 1 red onion, thinly sliced
- 2 tablespoons Cajun seasoning
- 1 teaspoon cumin
- 1 teaspoon chili powder
- 2 tablespoons olive oil
- 8 small whole wheat tortillas
- Guacamole, salsa, and vegan sour cream for serving

Directions:

1. Toss the chickpeas, bell peppers, red onion, cumin, and chili powder together in a bowl. Cajun seasoning should also be added.
2. Sauté the chickpea combination in a skillet that has been heated with olive oil until the vegetables are soft, which should take around 15 minutes.
3. Tortillas should be warmed in a dry pan.
4. To make fajitas, combine the chickpea mixture with the meat. Serve with vegan sour cream, salsa, and guacamole as accompaniments.

183.   VEGAN RED BEAN GOULASH

Total Time: 1 hour

Prep Time: 15 minutes

Ingredients:

- 2 cups cooked red beans
- 1 large onion, diced
- 2 bell peppers, diced
- 3 cloves garlic, minced
- 2 tablespoons Cajun seasoning
- 1 teaspoon thyme
- 1 teaspoon smoked paprika
- 1 can (14 oz) diced tomatoes
- 2 cups vegetable broth
- Salt and pepper to taste
- Cooked rice for serving

Directions:

1. To soften the onions, bell peppers, and garlic, sauté them in a large saucepan until they are tender.
2. Incorporate smoked paprika, thyme, Cajun flavor, and red beans into the mixture. Give it a good stir.
3. To the pot, add chopped tomatoes and broth made from vegetables. Allow it to cook for thirty to forty minutes after bringing it to a simmer.
4. Before seasoning with salt, add pepper and salt to taste.
5. While the rice is cooking, serve.

184.   RED PEPPER AND ARTICHOKE GRITS WRAPS

Total Time: 45 minutes

Prep Time: 20 minutes

Ingredients:

- 1 cup grits
- 4 cups water
- 1 cup almond milk
- Salt and pepper to taste
- 1 cup roasted red peppers, sliced

- 1 cup marinated artichoke hearts, chopped
- 1 cup spinach, chopped
- 8 whole wheat wraps

Directions:

1. Follow the package directions to make the grits using water and almond milk. Season the meat with salt and pepper.
2. Each wrap made from whole wheat should have a layer of cooked grits spread over it.
3. The toppings should consist of spinach, artichoke hearts, and roasted red peppers.
4. In the event that toothpicks are required, roll up the wrappers and fasten them.
5. The dish can be served immediately or warmed in a skillet before being used.

185.   BLACKENED TEMPEH CAESAR SALAD WRAPS

Total Time: 30 minutes

Prep Time: 15 minutes

Ingredients:

- 1 package of tempeh, sliced
- 2 tablespoons Cajun seasoning
- 1 tablespoon olive oil

- 4 whole-grain wraps
- 1 head of romaine lettuce, chopped
- 1 cup cherry tomatoes, halved
- 1/2 cup vegan Caesar dressing
- Salt and pepper to taste

Directions:

1. In a bowl, combine the Cajun spice, salt, and pepper, and then apply it to the tempeh pieces.
2. Get the olive oil heated up to medium-high in a skillet. Until the tempeh slices are blackened, cook them for three to four minutes on each side.
3. The wraps may be warmed up in the microwave or in a pan.
4. Putting together wraps involves stuffing each wrap with a bit of blackened tempeh, chopped lettuce, and cherry tomatoes once they have been assembled.
5. Using vegan Caesar dressing, drizzle the dish, and then securely wrap it. Serve as soon as possible.

186.   CAJUN-STYLE VEGAN MAC AND CHEESE

Total Time: 45 minutes

Prep Time: 15 minutes

Ingredients:

- 2 cups elbow macaroni
- 2 cups peeled and diced potatoes
- 1 cup diced carrots
- 1/2 cup cashews, soaked
- 1/3 cup nutritional yeast
- 1/4 cup olive oil

- 2 cloves garlic, minced
- 1 teaspoon Cajun seasoning
- Salt and pepper to taste
- Chopped green onions for garnish (optional)

Directions:

1. Make macaroni in accordance with the directions on the box. Drain, then keep away for later use.
2. Potatoes and carrots should be boiled in a saucepan until they are soft. Extract the liquid and place it in a blender.
3. To the blender, add cashews that have been soaked, nutritional yeast, olive oil, garlic, Cajun spice, salt, and pepper. Blend until smooth. Blend until it is completely smooth.
4. Mix the macaroni that has been cooked with the cheese sauce.
5. If desired, garnish with green onions that have been chopped. Serve when still heated.

187. CAJUN COLLARD GREENS

Total Time: 40 minutes

Prep Time: 15 minutes

Ingredients:

- 1 bunch of collard greens, stems removed and leaves chopped
- 1 tablespoon olive oil
- 1 onion, finely chopped
- 2 cloves garlic, minced
- 1 teaspoon Cajun seasoning
- 1/2 teaspoon smoked paprika
- 1 cup vegetable broth
- Salt and pepper to taste
- Hot sauce for serving (optional)

Directions:

1. Reach medium heat in a big pot with the olive oil.
2. Sauté the onions and garlic until they have become more tender.
3. The Cajun spice and smoked paprika should be stirred in.
4. Cook the collard greens until they have become wilted.
5. Add the vegetable broth, then lower the heat and let it boil for twenty to twenty-five minutes.
6. Use pepper and salt to season the food. To serve, serve hot with spicy sauce if desired.

188.   CREOLE PUMPKIN BISQUE

Total Time: 50 minutes

Prep Time: 15 minutes

Ingredients:

- 2 tablespoons olive oil
- 1 onion, chopped
- 2 cloves garlic, minced
- 1 can (15 oz) pumpkin puree
- 4 cups vegetable broth
- 1 cup coconut milk
- 1 teaspoon Creole seasoning
- 1/2 teaspoon thyme
- Salt and pepper to taste
- Pumpkin seeds for garnish (optional)

Directions:

1. The onions and garlic should be cooked in olive oil in a big saucepan until they become transparent.
2. Pumpkin puree, vegetable broth, coconut milk, Creole spice, thyme, salt, and pepper could be added to the mixture if desired. Give it a good stir.
3. Bring to a simmer, then let it cook for thirty to thirty-five minutes.
4. To get a smooth consistency, purée the soup using an immersion blender.
5. To serve, bring to a boil and, if preferred, garnish with pumpkin seeds.

189.   CAJUN-STYLE STUFFED GRAPE LEAVES

Total Time: 1 hour 30 minutes

Prep Time: 45 minutes

Ingredients:

- 1 cup jasmine rice, uncooked
- 1 can (15 oz) chickpeas, drained and mashed
- 1/4 cup diced tomatoes
- 1/4 cup chopped green onions
- 2 tablespoons chopped fresh parsley
- 2 tablespoons Cajun seasoning
- 1 tablespoon olive oil
- 1 jar grape leaves, rinsed and drained

Directions:

1. Cook the jasmine rice in accordance with the directions on the package.
2. Rice that has been cooked, chickpeas that have been mashed, chopped tomatoes, green onions, parsley, Cajun spice, and olive oil should be mixed together in a big bowl. Combine thoroughly.
3. One grape leaf should be used, a spoonful of the mixture should be placed in the middle of the leaf, and the edges should be folded over the filling. Compactly roll up.
4. Carry on until each and every grape leaf has been packed.
5. Put the grape leaves that have been put into a steamer basket and let them steam for half an hour.
6. Before serving, let the dish gently cool down.

190.   CAJUN CORNBREAD STUFFING

Total Time: 1 hour

Prep Time: 20 minutes

Ingredients:

- 6 cups cornbread, crumbled
- 1 cup celery, finely chopped
- 1 cup onion, finely chopped
- 1 cup bell pepper, diced
- 2 cloves garlic, minced

- 1 cup vegetable broth
- 2 tablespoons Cajun seasoning
- 1/4 cup fresh parsley, chopped
- Salt and pepper to taste

Directions:

1. First, get your oven up to 175 degrees Celsius (or 350 degrees Fahrenheit).
2. Put the crumbled cornbread, celery, onion, bell pepper, and garlic into a large bowl and mix those ingredients together.
3. Vegetable broth, Cajun spice, parsley, salt, and pepper should be added to the mixture, after thoroughly combining, mix.
4. After the mixture has been transferred to a baking dish, bake it for forty minutes or until the top is golden brown colored.
5. Wait a few minutes before serving so that the dish may cool down.

191.   SWEET POTATO AND CHICKPEA GRITS BOWL

Total Time: 45 minutes

Prep Time: 15 minutes

Ingredients:

- 1 cup stone-ground grits
- 2 cups sweet potatoes, diced
- 1 can (15 oz) chickpeas, rinsed and drained

- 1 cup kale, chopped
- 1 tablespoon Cajun seasoning
- 2 tablespoons olive oil
- Salt and pepper to taste

Directions:

1. Cook the grits in accordance with the directions on the box.
2. In a pan over medium heat, warm the olive oil to prepare it.
3. First, get your oven up to 175 degrees Celsius (or 350 degrees Fahrenheit).
4. Chickpeas, kale, Cajun spice, salt, and pepper should be added to the dish. Cook the chickpeas until they are completely warm, and the kale has become wilted.
5. The sweet potato and chickpea combination should be served on top of a bed of grits that have been cooked.

192. VEGAN ZYDECO ZUCCHINI NOODLE STIR-FRY

Total Time: 30 minutes

Prep Time: 15 minutes

Ingredients:

- 4 zucchinis, spiralized
- 1 cup bell peppers, thinly sliced
- 1 cup cherry tomatoes, halved
- 1 cup okra, sliced
- 1/2 cup red onion, thinly sliced
- 3 cloves garlic, minced
- 2 tablespoons Cajun seasoning
- 2 tablespoons soy sauce
- 1 tablespoon olive oil
- Green onions for garnish

Directions:

1. In a pan over medium heat, warm the olive oil to prepare it.
2. Garlic, red onion, bell peppers, cherry tomatoes, and okra should be added to the dish. Stir-fry the veggies for five to seven minutes or until they are crisp-tender.
3. Incorporate soy sauce, Cajun flavor, and zucchini noodles into the dish. Keep stirring for a further three to five minutes.
4. Green onions should be used as a garnish before serving.

193.   DIRTY RICE AND VEGGIE SAUSAGE

Total Time: 45 minutes

Prep Time: 15 minutes

Ingredients:

- 1 cup long-grain white rice
- 1 tablespoon olive oil
- 1 onion, finely chopped
- 1 bell pepper, diced
- 2 celery stalks, finely chopped
- 2 cloves garlic, minced
- 1 package (12 oz) vegan sausage, sliced
- 1 teaspoon paprika
- 1 teaspoon thyme
- 1 teaspoon cayenne pepper (adjust to taste)
- Salt and black pepper to taste
- 2 green onions, chopped (for garnish)

Directions:

1. Prepare the rice in accordance with the directions on the package.
2. In a pan over medium heat, warm the olive oil to prepare it.
3. Celery, onions, and bell peppers should be added. For veggies to become more tender, sauté them.
4. Put some garlic in the skillet, and then add some sliced vegan sausage. Cook the sausage until it has a browned appearance.
5. Paprika, thyme, cayenne pepper, salt, and black pepper should be stirred in the mixture.
6. Add the rice to the skillet once it has finished cooking, and be sure to thoroughly combine it with the meat and veggies.
7. Continuing to cook for a further five to seven minutes will allow the flavors to combine. If it is required, adjust the seasoning.
8. Prior to serving, garnish with green onions that have been chopped.

194.   CAJUN CHICKPEA AND SPINACH STEW

Total Time: 30 minutes

Prep Time: 10 minutes

Ingredients:

- 2 tablespoons olive oil
- 1 onion, diced
- 3 cloves garlic, minced
- 1 can (15 oz) chickpeas, drained and rinsed
- 1 can (14 oz) diced tomatoes

- 1 teaspoon Cajun seasoning
- 1 teaspoon smoked paprika
- 1/2 teaspoon thyme
- Salt and black pepper to taste
- 4 cups fresh spinach

Directions:

1. Reach medium heat in a big pot with the olive oil. Sauté the onions and garlic until they have become more tender.
2. Cajun seasoning, smoked paprika, thyme, salt, and black pepper should be added to the mixture, along with chickpeas and chopped tomatoes. In order to mix, stir.
3. Allow the stew to boil for fifteen to twenty minutes, stirring it around every so often.
4. Put in some fresh spinach and let it simmer until it wilts.
5. To taste, adjust the spice, and serve the dish hot.

195. CREOLE THREE-BEAN CHILI

Total Time: 1 hour

Prep Time: 15 minutes

Ingredients:

- 1 tablespoon vegetable oil
- 1 onion, chopped
- 3 cloves garlic, minced
- 1 can (15 oz) black beans, drained and rinsed
- 1 can (15 oz) kidney beans, drained and rinsed
- 1 can (15 oz) pinto beans, drained and rinsed
- 1 can (14 oz) diced tomatoes
- 1 cup vegetable broth
- 2 tablespoons tomato paste
- 2 teaspoons Creole seasoning
- 1 teaspoon cumin
- 1/2 teaspoon smoked paprika
- Salt and black pepper to taste

Directions:

1. In a large saucepan, bring the vegetable oil to a temperature of medium. Sauté the onions and garlic until they have become more tender.
2. The following ingredients should be added: chopped tomatoes, black beans, kidney beans, pinto beans, tomato paste, and vegetable broth. In order to mix, stir.
3. Creole seasoning, cumin, smoked paprika, salt, and black pepper should be used to complete the seasoning. Combine thoroughly.
4. Chili should be simmered for 45 minutes after it boils, with stirring every so often.
5. To taste, adjust the spice, and serve the dish hot.

196. VEGAN RED BEANS AND RICE

Total Time: 1 hour 15 minutes

Prep Time: 20 minutes

Ingredients:

- 1 cup dried red kidney beans, soaked overnight
- 2 tablespoons vegetable oil
- 1 onion, finely chopped
- 2 celery stalks, finely chopped
- 1 bell pepper, diced
- 3 cloves garlic, minced
- 1 teaspoon thyme
- 2 bay leaves
- 1 teaspoon smoked paprika
- 1 teaspoon Cajun seasoning
- Salt and black pepper to taste
- 4 cups cooked white rice

Directions:

1. Take the kidney beans that have been soaked and cook them in a saucepan until they are soft.
2. Prepare the vegetable oil by heating it in a large pan over medium heat. The bell pepper, onions, and celery should be added. For veggies to become more tender, sauté them.
3. Add the following Ingredients: smoked paprika, garlic, thyme, bay leaves, Cajun spice, salt, and black pepper. In order to mix, stir.
4. After adding the kidney beans that have been cooked, continue to boil for an additional 15–20 minutes.
5. Serve the red beans on top of a bed of white rice that has been cooked.

197. CAJUN-STYLE VEGAN DIRTY QUINOA

Total Time: 40 minutes

Prep Time: 15 minutes

Ingredients:

- 1 cup quinoa
- 2 cups vegetable broth
- 1 tablespoon olive oil
- 1 onion, finely chopped
- 2 celery stalks, diced
- 1 bell pepper, diced
- 3 cloves garlic, minced
- 1 can (15 oz) black-eyed peas, drained and rinsed
- 1 teaspoon Cajun seasoning
- 1/2 teaspoon smoked paprika
- Salt and pepper to taste
- Green onions, chopped (for garnish)

Directions:

1. The quinoa should be washed in cold water. Combining quinoa and vegetable broth in a pot is the first step. The quinoa should be prepared by bringing it to a boil, then lowering the heat, covering it, and simmering it for fifteen to twenty minutes.
2. Get the olive oil ready by warming it in a big pan over medium heat. Add the bell pepper, onion, and celery to the pan. For veggies to become more tender, sauté them.
3. In a pan, whisk together the following *Ingredients:* minced garlic, black-eyed peas, Cajun spice, smoked paprika, salt, and pepper. Wait an extra five minutes before serving.
4. Stir in the quinoa that has been cooked, ensuring that all of the ingredients are fully combined. Wait an extra five minutes before serving.
5. Prior to serving, garnish with green onions that have been chopped. I hope you like your vegan dirty quinoa in a Cajun style!

198. RED PEPPER AND CORN MAQUE CHOUX

Total Time: 30 minutes

Prep Time: 10 minutes

Ingredients:

- 2 tablespoons olive oil
- 1 onion, finely chopped
- 1 red bell pepper, diced
- 1 cup corn kernels
- 2 tomatoes, diced
- 2 cloves garlic, minced

- 1 teaspoon thyme
- 1 teaspoon paprika
- Salt and pepper to taste
- Fresh parsley, chopped (for garnish)

Directions:

1. To get the olive oil ready, heat it in a big pan over medium heat. Include chopped onion and red bell pepper in the list. Sauté the veggies until they have become more tender.
2. In the skillet, combine the following *Ingredients:* corn, diced tomatoes, minced garlic, thyme, paprika, salt, and pepper. Cook for approximately fifteen minutes, stirring the mixture each time.
3. After the veggies have reached the desired level of tenderness, remove them from the fire. Immediately prior to serving, garnish with fresh parsley. I hope you like this Maque Choux with Red Pepper and Corn!

199. VEGAN MARDI GRAS MUFFINS

Total Time: 45 minutes

Prep Time: 20 minutes

Ingredients:

- 2 cups all-purpose flour
- 1 cup sugar
- 1 tablespoon baking powder
- 1/2 teaspoon salt
- 1 cup mashed bananas
- 1/2 cup applesauce
- 1/2 cup vegetable oil
- 1 teaspoon vanilla extract
- 1/2 cup chopped pecans
- 1/2 cup shredded coconut
- Vegan cream cheese (optional for topping)

Directions:

1. Before you even think about placing the muffin pan in the oven, get the temperature up to 350 degrees Fahrenheit (175 degrees Celsius).
2. Divide the applesauce, bananas, vegetable oil, and vanilla essence into two bowls and stir them together.
3. Once the dry ingredients are nearly combined, pour in the wet components and whisk to combine. Now is the time to mix in the pecans and shredded coconut.
4. To make muffins, spoon batter into a muffin pan. Add a toothpick and bake for 20 to 25 minutes or until the center comes out clean.
5. It is recommended that you wait until the muffins have cooled before topping them with vegan cream cheese. I hope you enjoy your vegan treat for Mardi Gras!

200. CAJUN CAULIFLOWER AND CHICKPEA TACOS

Total Time: 35 minutes

Prep Time: 15 minutes

Ingredients:

- 1 small head cauliflower, cut into florets
- 1 can (15 oz) chickpeas, drained and rinsed
- 2 tablespoons Cajun seasoning
- 1 tablespoon olive oil
- 1 lime, juiced
- 1/2 cup vegan coleslaw mix
- 8 small corn tortillas
- Avocado slices (for garnish)
- Fresh cilantro (for garnish)

Directions:

1. Roast the vegetables until they are soft, about 20 minutes before serving.
2. Cajun spice, olive oil, and lime juice should be mixed together in a big dish and then transferred to cauliflower florets and chickpeas.
3. Position the mixture of chickpeas and cauliflower on a baking sheet and spread it out. Roast for twenty to twenty-five minutes or until toasty and crunchy.
4. Either a dry skillet or the microwave may be used to warm the corn tortillas.
5. In order to assemble the tacos, fill each tortilla with a combination of roasted cauliflower and chickpeas. The vegan coleslaw, avocado slices, and fresh cilantro are the toppings for this dish.
6. Cajun Cauliflower and Chickpea Tacos are ready to be served immediately, and you may enjoy them!

201. ZESTY CAJUN STUFFED POBLANO PEPPERS

Total Time: 1 hour 15 minutes

Prep Time: 30 minutes

Ingredients:

- 4 large poblano peppers
- 1 cup cooked black beans
- 1 cup cooked brown rice
- 1 cup corn kernels
- 1 cup diced tomatoes
- 1/2 cup diced red onion

- 2 cloves garlic, minced
- 1 teaspoon Cajun seasoning
- 1 teaspoon smoked paprika
- Salt and pepper to taste
- 1 cup vegan shredded cheese
- Fresh cilantro for garnish

Directions:

1. Position the oven dial to 375 °F, which is equivalent to 190 °C.
2. After removing the poblano peppers' seeds and membranes, slice off their tops.
3. In a large bowl, combine the following *Ingredients:* black beans, brown rice, corn, tomatoes, red onion, garlic, Cajun spice, smoked paprika, salt, and pepper. Mix for two minutes.
4. Prepare a baking dish and then stuff each poblano pepper with the mixture. Place the peppers in the dish.
5. Shredded vegan cheese should be sprinkled on top of each pepper that has been packed.
6. In an oven that has been warmed, bake the peppers for forty-five to fifty minutes or until they are soft and the cheese has melted and become bubbly.
7. Fresh cilantro should be used as a garnish before serving.

202.   VEGAN MARDI GRAS POPCORN

Total Time: 15 minutes

Prep Time: 5 minutes

Ingredients:

- 1/2 cup popcorn kernels
- 3 tablespoons vegan butter, melted
- One tablespoon of Cajun seasoning
- 1 teaspoon garlic powder
- 1/2 teaspoon onion powder
- 1/2 teaspoon smoked paprika
- Salt to taste

Directions:

1. The popcorn kernels should be popped in accordance with the directions on the packaging.
2. All of the following ingredients should be combined in a small bowl: melted vegan butter, Cajun spice, garlic powder, onion powder, smoky paprika, and salt.
3. Apply the spice mixture to the popcorn that has been popped, and then toss it so that it is equally coated.
4. You should serve it right away, and you should enjoy your vegan Mardi Gras popcorn!

203. QUINOA AND KALE JAMBALAYA

Total Time: 45 minutes

Prep Time: 15 minutes

Ingredients:

- 1 cup quinoa, rinsed and drained
- 2 cups vegetable broth
- 1 tablespoon olive oil
- 1 onion, diced
- 2 bell peppers, diced
- 3 cloves garlic, minced
- 1 teaspoon Cajun seasoning
- 1 teaspoon thyme
- 1/2 teaspoon smoked paprika
- 1 can (15 oz) diced tomatoes
- 3 cups chopped kale
- Salt and pepper to taste
- Green onions for garnish

Directions:

1. Quinoa and vegetable broth should be mixed together in a medium-sized pot. Cook the quinoa and soak up the liquid by reducing the heat to low, covering the saucepan, and simmering for fifteen to twenty minutes after it boils.
2. Make sure that the olive oil is brought to a simmer in a big saucepan that is set over medium heat before it is used. The garlic, onion, and bell peppers should be added. Sauté the veggies until they become more tender.
3. Cajun spice, thyme, smoked paprika, diced tomatoes, and chopped kale should be stirred in at this point. Cook the kale until it has become wilted.
4. Take the quinoa that has been cooked and add it to the skillet. Add pepper and salt to taste, and season with salt when you are done.
5. Prior to serving, garnish with green onions that have been chopped.

204. CAJUN CABBAGE ROLLS

Total Time: 1 hour 30 minutes

Prep Time: 45 minutes

Ingredients:

- 1 large head of cabbage
- 1 cup cooked white rice
- 1 cup lentils, cooked
- 1 onion, finely chopped
- 2 cloves garlic, minced
- 1 can (15 oz) tomato sauce
- 1 teaspoon Cajun seasoning
- 1/2 teaspoon thyme
- 1/2 teaspoon oregano
- Salt and pepper to taste
- Chopped parsley for garnish

Directions:

1. Before baking, preheat the oven to 175 degrees Celsius (350 degrees F.
2. The water in a big saucepan should be brought to a boil. The entire head of cabbage should be submerged in water and boiled for five to seven minutes or until the leaves become tender and flexible.
3. Cooked rice, lentils, onion, garlic, Cajun spice, thyme, oregano, salt, and pepper should be mixed together in a basin before being added to the mixture.
4. A teaspoon of the filling should be placed into each cabbage leaf once the leaves have been carefully peeled off. To bake them, roll them up and set them in a baking tray with the seam side down.
5. Combine tomato sauce and more Cajun spice in a bowl and well combine. Coat the cabbage rolls with the sauce and set them off.
6. Bake for forty-five to fifty minutes with the baking dish covered with aluminum foil.
7. Before serving, garnish with chopped parsley from the garden.

205. CAJUN-STYLE VEGAN GRITS AND GREENS

Total Time: 30 minutes

Prep Time: 10 minutes

Ingredients:

- 1 cup grits
- 4 cups water
- 2 cups chopped collard greens
- 1 tablespoon olive oil
- 1 onion, finely chopped

- 2 cloves garlic, minced
- 1 bell pepper, diced
- 1 teaspoon Cajun seasoning
- Salt and pepper to taste
- Green onions for garnish

Directions:

1. The water should be brought to a boil in a saucepan. Whisk the grits in slowly, then decrease the heat to low, cover the pot, and let it simmer for twenty minutes while stirring it periodically.
2. Prepare the olive oil in a separate skillet by heating it over medium heat. To the pan, add the bell pepper, onions, and garlic. To ensure that the veggies are cooked through.
3. Cajun spice, salt, and pepper should be mixed in with the collard greens. Wait until the greens have become wilted.
4. A combination of the greens and the grits should be combined. After thorough mixing, continue to cook for an additional five minutes.
5. Serve while still hot, with green onions as a garnish.

206.   VEGAN RED BEAN AND COLLARD GREEN TACOS

Total Time: 25 minutes

Prep Time: 15 minutes

Ingredients:

- 1 can (15 oz) red beans, drained and rinsed
- 2 cups chopped collard greens
- 1 tablespoon olive oil
- 1 teaspoon Cajun seasoning
- 8 small corn tortillas
- Avocado slices for topping
- Salsa for garnish

Directions:

1. The olive oil should be heated in a pan over medium heat. Sauté the collard greens until they have become wilted.
2. The pan should be seasoned with Cajun spice and red beans. Prepare the beans until they are completely warm.
3. You may reheat tortillas in the microwave or in a dry skillet.
4. Place a dollop of the mixture consisting of red beans and collard greens onto each tortilla.
5. Avocado slices and salsa should be placed on top.
6. Serve as soon as possible.

207. JAZZY JACKFRUIT TOSTADAS

Total Time: 40 minutes

Prep Time: 20 minutes

Ingredients:

- 1 can (20 oz) young jackfruit, drained and shredded
- 2 tablespoons Cajun seasoning
- 1 tablespoon olive oil
- 8 tostada shells
- Vegan sour cream for topping
- Chopped cilantro for garnish
- Lime wedges for serving

Directions:

1. Gather the olive oil and heat it in a skillet over medium heat.
2. Include Cajun spice and shredded jackfruit in the dish. The jackfruit should be cooked until it is soft and evenly coated.
3. Tostada shells should be warmed in the oven while the jackfruit is cooking.
4. Tostada shells should be topped with the jackfruit that has been seasoned.
5. Place some vegan sour cream on top, and then sprinkle some chopped cilantro on those.
6. Lime wedges should be served on the side.

208.   VEGAN RED BEAN HUMMUS

Total Time: 10 minutes

Prep Time: 10 minutes

Ingredients:

- 1 can (15 oz) red beans, drained and rinsed
- 2 cloves garlic
- 1/4 cup tahini
- 2 tablespoons olive oil
- 2 tablespoons lemon juice
- 1 teaspoon Cajun seasoning
- Salt and pepper to taste
- Pita bread or vegetable sticks for serving

Directions:

1. Put the red beans, garlic, tahini, olive oil, lemon juice, and Cajun spice into a food processor and pulse until everything is combined.
2. Blend until smooth, paying attention to the edges of the bowl as necessary.
3. Add pepper and salt to taste, and season with salt when you are done.
4. Please adjust the Cajun seasoning to your liking.
5. Move the mixture to a bowl for serving, and then sprinkle it with more olive oil.
6. To accompany, pita bread or veggie sticks might be served.

209.   VEGAN ALLIGATOR GUMBO

Total Time: 1 hour 30 minutes

Prep Time: 30 minutes

Ingredients:

- 1 cup okra, sliced
- 1 cup bell peppers, diced
- 1 cup celery, chopped
- 1 cup onion, finely chopped
- 3 cloves garlic, minced
- 2 tablespoons vegetable oil
- 1 cup vegan sausage, sliced
- 1 cup vegan chicken substitute, diced
- 1/2 cup all-purpose flour
- 4 cups vegetable broth
- 1 can (14 oz) diced tomatoes
- 1 teaspoon Cajun seasoning
- 1/2 teaspoon thyme
- 1 bay leaf
- Salt and pepper to taste
- 2 cups cooked white rice
- Green onions for garnish

Directions:

1. Keep the vegetable oil warm by heating it in a big saucepan over medium heat. In order to form a roux, adding the flour and stirring it constantly until it gets a dark brown hue is the first step.
2. Include the garlic, onion, celery, and bell peppers in the mixture. The veggies should be sautéed until they are soft.
3. The vegan sausage and chicken replacement should be stirred in and allowed to brown slightly before being added.
4. Incorporate the chopped tomatoes and veggie broth into the mixture. Okra, Cajun spice, thyme, bay leaf, salt, and pepper should be added to the mixture. Allow to come to a simmer.
5. While stirring it occasionally, reduce the heat to low and allow the gumbo to simmer for forty-five to sixty minutes.
6. Serve the gumbo on top of a bed of white rice that has been cooked. Add some green onions as a decorator.

210.   VEGAN HUSHPUPPIES WITH JALAPEÑO AIOLI

Total Time: 45 minutes

Prep Time: 15 minutes

Ingredients:

- 1 cup cornmeal
- 1/2 cup all-purpose flour
- 1 teaspoon baking powder
- 1/2 teaspoon baking soda
- 1/2 teaspoon salt
- 1 cup corn kernels
- 1/4 cup green onions, finely chopped
- 1 cup non-dairy milk
- Vegetable oil for frying
- For Jalapeño Aioli:
- 1/2 cup vegan mayonnaise
- 1 tablespoon fresh jalapeño, minced
- 1 tablespoon lemon juice
- Salt and pepper to taste

Directions:

1. Get a bowl and combine the cornmeal, flour, baking powder, baking soda, and salt.
2. After stirring in the non-dairy milk, corn kernels, and green onions, the mixture should be just blended.
3. A large pot or deep fryer should be heated to 175 degrees Celsius (350 degrees Fahrenheit) for the vegetable oil.
4. The batter should be dropped by spoonfuls into the heated oil and fried until it is golden brown, flipping it over as necessary. Using paper towels, drain the liquid.
5. To make the jalapeño aioli, combine vegan mayonnaise, minced jalapeño, lemon juice, salt, and pepper in a mixing bowl.
6. The hushpuppies should be served hot with jalapeño aioli being used for dipping.

211.   CAJUN RED LENTIL AND POTATO CURRY

Total Time: 40 minutes

Prep Time: 15 minutes

Ingredients:

- 1 cup red lentils, rinsed
- 2 cups potatoes, diced
- 1 onion, finely chopped
- 3 cloves garlic, minced
- 1 can (14 oz) coconut milk
- 1 can (14 oz) diced tomatoes
- 2 tablespoons Cajun seasoning
- 1 teaspoon cumin
- 1 teaspoon paprika
- 1/2 teaspoon cayenne pepper (optional)
- Salt and pepper to taste
- Fresh cilantro for garnish
- Cooked rice for serving

Directions:

1. Red lentils, potatoes, onion, garlic, coconut milk, chopped tomatoes, Cajun spice, cumin, paprika, cayenne pepper, salt, and pepper should be mixed together in a saucepan.
2. The potatoes and lentils should be cooked until they are soft, which should take around 25 to 30 minutes after returning to a boil.
3. Adjust the seasoning to your liking.
4. To serve, place on top of cooked rice and top with chopped fresh cilantro.

212.   RED PEPPER AND CORN MAQUE CHOUX SALAD

Total Time: 20 minutes

Prep Time: 10 minutes

Ingredients:

- 2 cups corn kernels
- 1 red bell pepper, diced
- 1/2 cup red onion, finely chopped
- 1/4 cup fresh parsley, chopped
- 2 tablespoons olive oil
- 1 tablespoon apple cider vinegar
- 1 teaspoon Cajun seasoning
- Salt and pepper to taste

Directions:

1. Put the corn, red bell pepper, red onion, and parsley into a big bowl and mix them together.
2. Olive oil, apple cider vinegar, Cajun spice, salt, and pepper should be mixed together in a small bowl after being whisked together.
3. Once the dressing has been poured over the corn mixture, toss it until it is evenly covered.
4. Prior to serving, allow the dish to chill in the refrigerator for a minimum of ten minutes.

213.   VEGAN PO' BOY TACOS

Total Time: 30 minutes

Prep Time: 15 minutes

Ingredients:

- 1 cup shredded green cabbage
- 1 cup shredded carrots
- 1 cup sliced tomatoes
- 1 cup sliced avocado
- 1 cup cooked and seasoned tofu, cubed

- 8 small corn tortillas
- 1/4 cup vegan mayo
- 2 tablespoons Cajun seasoning
- 2 tablespoons olive oil
- Salt and pepper to taste

Directions:

1. The shredded cabbage and carrots should be combined in a dish. Mix with some vegan mayonnaise, then set it aside.
2. A saucepan filled with olive oil should be heated to a simmer over medium heat. When the tofu cubes have reached a golden brown color, add them to the pan.
3. Prepare the corn tortillas by heating them in a microwave or a dry pan.
4. Putting together tacos involves spreading a layer of the cabbage-carrot mixture on each tortilla, then topping it with tofu cubes, sliced tomatoes, avocado, and Cajun spice.
5. Salt and pepper should be added to taste. Serve right away, and savor the deliciousness of your vegan po' boy tacos!

214. CAJUN STUFFED ACORN SQUASH

Total Time: 1 hour

Prep Time: 20 minutes

Ingredients:

- 2 acorn squash, halved and seeds removed
- 1 cup cooked quinoa
- 1 cup black beans, drained and rinsed
- 1 cup corn kernels
- 1 cup diced bell peppers (assorted colors)
- 1/2 cup diced red onion
- 2 cloves garlic, minced
- 2 tablespoons Cajun seasoning
- 2 tablespoons olive oil
- Salt and pepper to taste
- Fresh cilantro for garnish

Directions:

1. Roast the vegetables until they are soft, about 20 minutes before serving.
2. Arrange the acorn squash halves and cut sides up on a baking sheet. Salt should be sprinkled on top of the olive oil brushed on. Roast for forty to forty-five minutes or until the meat is tender.
3. Combine the quinoa that has been cooked, the black beans, the corn, the bell peppers, the red onion, the garlic, the Cajun spice, and the olive oil in a large bowl. Combine thoroughly.
4. When the squash is done cooking, put the quinoa mixture into each side of the squash.
5. Place back into the oven and continue baking for another ten to fifteen minutes.
6. Fresh cilantro should be used as a garnish before serving. Enjoy your stuffed acorn squash with a Cajun flavor!

215. SPICY CAJUN SWEET POTATO FRITTERS

Total Time: 45 minutes

Prep Time: 20 minutes

Ingredients:

- 2 large sweet potatoes, grated
- 1 cup chickpea flour
- 1/4 cup chopped green onions
- 2 tablespoons Cajun seasoning
- 1 teaspoon baking powder
- 1/2 teaspoon salt
- 1/4 teaspoon black pepper
- 1/4 cup water
- Vegetable oil for frying

Directions:

1. Sweet potatoes that have been grated, chickpea flour, green onions, Cajun spice, baking powder, salt, and black pepper should be mixed together in a big basin.
2. To create a thick batter, gradually add water to the mixture.
3. While the stove is on medium heat, gently simmer the vegetable oil.
4. Fritters are formed by spooning parts of the batter into the heated oil and shaping them into little balls. To get a golden brown color on both sides, fry.
5. Take the object out of the oil and lay it on paper towels so that the excess oil may settle.
6. Keep the food hot and crisp. Your Spicy Cajun Sweet Potato Fritters are ready to be enjoyed!

216. VEGAN CREOLE EGGPLANT

Total Time: 40 minutes

Prep Time: 15 minutes

Ingredients:

- 2 large eggplants, sliced into rounds
- 1 cup tomato sauce
- 1 cup diced bell peppers (assorted colors)
- 1 cup diced onions
- 3 cloves garlic, minced
- 2 tablespoons Cajun seasoning
- 2 tablespoons olive oil
- Salt and pepper to taste
- Chopped parsley for garnish

Directions:

1. Get the oven hot, about 190 degrees Celsius (375 degrees Fahrenheit).
2. The eggplant slices should be placed on a baking pan. Salt should be sprinkled on both sides after the olive oil has been brushed on.
3. Bake for twenty to twenty-five minutes or until the top is golden brown.
4. While the onions, bell peppers, and garlic are softening, put them in a skillet and sauté them in olive oil.
5. Cajun seasoning and tomato sauce should be added to the mixture. Reduce heat and simmer for 10 minutes.
6. Place the roasted eggplant slices on a serving platter and top with the Creole sauce.
7. Before serving hot, garnish with chopped parsley. Veggie creole eggplant is delicious, so savor every bite!

217. JAZZY JACKFRUIT ENCHILADAS

Total Time: 1 hour 15 minutes

Prep Time: 30 minutes

Ingredients:

- 2 cans (20 oz each) young jackfruit, drained and shredded
- 1 large onion, diced
- 2 cloves garlic, minced
- 1 bell pepper, chopped
- 1 cup corn kernels
- 1 can (15 oz) black beans, drained and rinsed

- 1 cup enchilada sauce
- 1 teaspoon cumin
- 1 teaspoon smoked paprika
- 1 teaspoon chili powder
- Salt and pepper to taste
- 8 large tortillas
- 1 cup vegan cheese, shredded
- Fresh cilantro for garnish

Directions:

1. Get the oven hot, about 190 degrees Celsius (375 degrees Fahrenheit).
2. Place the onion and garlic in a big pan and sauté them until they become transparent.
3. The jackfruit, bell pepper, maize, black beans, cumin, smoked paprika, chili powder, salt, and pepper should be added together with the other ingredients. To ensure that the jackfruit is soft, cook it for ten to fifteen minutes.
4. The jackfruit mixture should be stuffed into each tortilla once it has been warmed. To bake them, roll them up and set them in a baking tray with the seam side down.
5. Following the rolling of the tortillas, pour the enchilada sauce over them and top them with vegan cheese.
6. In an oven that has been warmed, bake the cheese for twenty-five to thirty minutes or until it is melted and bubbling.
7. Fresh cilantro should be used as a garnish before serving.

218.   VEGAN BAYOU BURGERS

Total Time: 45 minutes

Prep Time: 15 minutes

Ingredients:

- 2 cups black beans, cooked and mashed
- 1 cup breadcrumbs
- 1 small red onion, finely chopped
- 2 cloves garlic, minced
- 1 tablespoon Cajun seasoning
- 1 tablespoon soy sauce
- 1 tablespoon olive oil
- 4 whole-grain burger buns
- Lettuce, tomato, and vegan mayo for toppings

Directions:

1. Blend together the following ingredients in a large bowl: breadcrumbs, mashed black beans, red onion, garlic, Cajun spice, and soy sauce. Combine thoroughly.
2. Burger patties should be formed from the ingredients.
3. Reduce heat to medium and bring olive oil to a simmer.
4. Cook each side of the burgers for four to five minutes or until they reach a golden brown color.
5. The burger buns should be toasted before being assembled with lettuce, tomato, and vegan mayonnaise.

219.   CAJUN COLLARD GREEN BURRITO BOWL

Total Time: 40 minutes

Prep Time: 20 minutes

Ingredients:

- 2 cups cooked quinoa
- 1 bunch collard greens, stems removed and chopped
- 1 cup cherry tomatoes, halved
- 1 cup corn kernels
- 1 avocado, sliced
- 1 can (15 oz) black beans, drained and rinsed
- Cajun dressing (mix olive oil, Cajun seasoning, and lemon juice)
- Salt and pepper to taste

Directions:

1. Collard greens should be cooked in a big pan until they become wilted. Use pepper and salt to season the food.
2. In each bowl, combine the following Ingredients: quinoa, collard greens that have been sautéed, cherry tomatoes, corn, black beans, and avocado slices.
3. Cajun dressing should be drizzled over the bowls before they are served.

220.   VEGAN GRITS AND AVOCADO TOAST

Total Time: 30 minutes

Prep Time: 15 minutes

Ingredients:

- 1 cup grits
- 4 cups water or vegetable broth
- Salt and pepper to taste

- 2 avocados, mashed
- Cherry tomatoes, sliced
- Red pepper flakes for garnish
- Whole-grain bread slices toasted

Directions:

1. Cook the grits in water or vegetable broth, as directed on the package, according to the directions. Use pepper and salt to season the food.
2. Please toast the pieces of bread.
3. Distribute mashed avocado on the bread that has been toasted.
4. The dish is finished off with a substantial amount of grits, cherry tomatoes that have been sliced, and a sprinkling of red pepper flakes.

221. SPICY QUINOA AND OKRA BOWL

Total Time: 30 minutes

Prep Time: 10 minutes

Ingredients:

- 1 cup quinoa, rinsed
- 2 cups vegetable broth
- 1 cup okra, sliced
- 1 can (15 oz) black beans, drained and rinsed
- 1 cup cherry tomatoes, halved
- 1 red bell pepper, diced
- 2 cloves garlic, minced
- 1 teaspoon Cajun seasoning
- 1/2 teaspoon smoked paprika
- Salt and pepper to taste
- 2 tablespoons olive oil
- Fresh parsley for garnish

Directions:

1. Create a boil in the vegetable broth by placing it in a medium-sized pot. Add the quinoa, then cover the pot, decrease the heat to low, and let it simmer for fifteen minutes or until the quinoa is cooked.
2. A big saucepan should be heated over medium heat in order to prepare the olive oil.
3. Sauté the garlic until it achieves a fragrant state.
4. To the pan, add the okra, black beans, cherry tomatoes, and red bell pepper. Serve immediately. When the veggies are soft, cook them for five to seven minutes.
5. This is the time to whisk in the cooked quinoa, Cajun seasoning, smoked paprika, salt, and pepper. Be sure to stir everything well so it can mingle.
6. Make sure everything is heated by cooking for two or three more minutes.
7. While still hot, garnish with chopped fresh parsley and serve. I hope you like your bowl of spicy quinoa and okra!

222. JAZZY JACKFRUIT JAMBALAYA

Total Time: 45 minutes

Prep Time: 15 minutes

Ingredients:

- 2 cups jasmine rice, cooked
- 1 can (20 oz) young jackfruit, drained and shredded
- 1 onion, diced
- 1 green bell pepper, diced
- 2 celery stalks, chopped
- 3 cloves garlic, minced
- 1 can (14 oz) diced tomatoes
- 1 cup vegetable broth
- 1 tablespoon Cajun seasoning
- 1 teaspoon dried thyme
- 1/2 teaspoon smoked paprika
- Salt and pepper to taste
- 2 tablespoons olive oil
- Fresh parsley for garnish

Directions:

1. To integrate the olive oil, first bring it to a warm temperature in a large pot over medium heat, and then whisk it. Include celery, green bell pepper, and onion in the dish. To soften the meat, sauté it.
2. Add shredded jackfruit and minced garlic to the pan and stir to combine. Cook the jackfruit for five to seven minutes or until it's browned.
3. The mixture should be stirred to incorporate the ingredients after adding chopped tomatoes, vegetable broth, Cajun spice, dried thyme, smoked paprika, salt, and pepper. Warm for fifteen to twenty minutes.
4. On top of the jasmine rice that has been cooked, serve the jambalaya.
5. Garnish with fresh parsley that has been chopped, and serve while it is still hot. I hope you like your Jambalaya with Jazzy Jackfruit!

223.   CREOLE TOFU SCRAMBLE

Total Time: 20 minutes

Prep Time: 10 minutes

Ingredients:

- 1 block (14 oz) firm tofu, crumbled
- 1 onion, finely chopped
- 1 bell pepper, diced
- 2 cloves garlic, minced
- 1 cup cherry tomatoes, halved
- 1 cup spinach, chopped
- 2 tablespoons nutritional yeast
- 1 teaspoon Cajun seasoning
- Salt and pepper to taste
- 2 tablespoons olive oil
- Fresh chives for garnish

Directions:

1. To integrate the olive oil, first bring it to a warm temperature in a large pot over medium heat, and then whisk it.
2. A diced onion and bell pepper should be added. To soften the meat, sauté it.
3. Add crumbled tofu and minced garlic to the pan and stir to combine. Allow to cook for five to seven minutes, stirring periodically.
4. Be sure to include the chopped spinach, cherry tomatoes, nutritional yeast, Cajun spice, salt, and pepper in the mixture. Continue to cook for an additional three to five minutes.
5. Top with chopped fresh chives, and serve while still hot. I hope you like your scrambled Creole tofu!

224. CAJUN QUINOA SALAD

Total Time: 25 minutes

Prep Time: 15 minutes

Ingredients:

- 2 cups cooked quinoa
- 1 can (15 oz) black-eyed peas, drained and rinsed
- 1 cup corn kernels, cooked
- 1 bell pepper, diced
- 1/2 red onion, finely chopped
- 1/4 cup fresh cilantro, chopped
- 1/4 cup olive oil
- 2 tablespoons apple cider vinegar
- 1 tablespoon Dijon mustard
- 1 teaspoon Cajun seasoning
- Salt and pepper to taste

Directions:

1. Combine the quinoa that has been cooked, the black-eyed peas, the corn, the bell pepper, the red onion, and the cilantro in a large bowl.
2. For the preparation of the Cajun seasoning, olive oil, apple cider vinegar, Dijon mustard, salt, and pepper, put all of the ingredients in a small bowl and mix them together in a gentle manner.
3. After the dressing has been poured over the quinoa mixture, toss it until it is thoroughly incorporated.
4. Prior to serving, allow the dish to chill in the refrigerator for a minimum of ten minutes. Wishing you a delicious Cajun Quinoa Salad!

225.   VEGAN BOUDIN BALLS

Total Time: 1 hour 30 minutes

Prep Time: 45 minutes

Ingredients:

- 2 cups cooked and cooled jasmine rice
- 1 cup cooked lentils, mashed
- 1 cup finely chopped mushrooms
- 1/2 cup diced bell peppers
- 1/4 cup finely chopped celery
- 2 cloves garlic, minced
- 1 teaspoon Cajun seasoning
- 1/2 teaspoon paprika
- Salt and pepper to taste
- 1 cup breadcrumbs
- 1 cup all-purpose flour
- 1 cup unsweetened almond milk
- Vegetable oil for frying

Directions:

1. Rice that has been cooked, lentils that have been mashed, mushrooms, bell peppers, celery, garlic, Cajun spice, paprika, salt, and pepper should all be mixed together in a big bowl.
2. After shaping the mixture into balls about the size of golf balls, set them aside.
3. The flour, the almond milk, and the breadcrumbs should each be placed in four separate dishes.
4. Once each ball has been coated with breadcrumbs, it should be rolled in flour and then dipped in almond milk.
5. A large pot or deep fryer should be heated to 175 degrees Celsius (350 degrees Fahrenheit) for the vegetable oil.
6. For approximately four to five minutes per batch, fry the boudin balls until they reach a golden brown color.
7. With the help of a slotted spoon, take the food from the pan and place it on a plate that has been lined with paper towels. Any extra oil can then be drained away in this way.
8. Warm the dish and serve it with the vegan dipping sauce of your choice.

226. VEGAN GUMBO WITH OKRA AND LENTILS

Total Time: 2 hours

Prep Time: 30 minutes

Ingredients:

- 1 cup dry green lentils, rinsed
- 4 cups vegetable broth
- 1 cup sliced okra
- 1 cup diced tomatoes
- 1 cup diced bell peppers
- 1 cup diced celery
- 1 cup diced onion

- 3 cloves garlic, minced
- 2 tablespoons vegetable oil
- 2 tablespoons all-purpose flour
- 1 tablespoon Cajun seasoning
- 1 teaspoon thyme
- Salt and pepper to taste
- Cooked rice for serving

Directions:

1. To make the lentils, mix them with the vegetable broth in a big saucepan. Lower the heat to a simmer and keep cooking for another 20 minutes after it boils.
2. In a separate pan, bring the oil to a medium temperature. A roux may be made by adding flour and stirring it continually. Continue to cook it until it reaches a dark brown color.
3. Include garlic, onion, bell peppers, and celery in the roux that you are making. Allow veggies to cook until they are soft.
4. The lentils should be seasoned with the roux-vegetable combination. Okra, tomatoes, Cajun spice, thyme, salt, and pepper should be stirred in at this point.
5. For a further forty to fifty minutes, continue to simmer the gumbo while tossing it periodically.
6. While the rice is cooking, serve.

227. SPICY CAJUN TEMPEH

Total Time: 45 minutes

Prep Time: 15 minutes

Ingredients:

- 1 package (8 oz) tempeh, sliced
- 2 tablespoons soy sauce
- 1 tablespoon olive oil
- 1 tablespoon Cajun seasoning
- 1 teaspoon smoked paprika
- 1 teaspoon garlic powder
- 1/2 teaspoon cayenne pepper (adjust to taste)
- 1 tablespoon maple syrup
- Lemon wedges for serving

Directions:

1. Get the oven hot, about 190 degrees Celsius (375 degrees Fahrenheit).
2. Soy sauce, olive oil, Cajun seasoning, smoked paprika, garlic powder, cayenne pepper, and maple syrup should all be mixed together in a bowl. Mixed well by whisking.
3. The marinade should be poured over the tempeh pieces that have been placed in a baking dish. Check to see that the tempeh is evenly covered.
4. The tempeh should be baked for twenty-five to thirty minutes, with a flip halfway through, until it is brown and crispy.
5. Please serve hot with slices of lemon.

228. RED PEPPER AND ARTICHOKE GRITS

Total Time: 45 minutes

Prep Time: 15 minutes

Ingredients:

- 1 cup grits
- 4 cups vegetable broth
- 1 cup diced red bell pepper
- 1 cup artichoke hearts, chopped
- 1/2 cup nutritional yeast
- 1/4 cup vegan butter
- Salt and pepper to taste
- Chopped green onions for garnish

Directions:

1. The vegetable broth should be brought to a boil in a saucepan. After gradually whisking in the grits, decrease the heat and continue to simmer until the mixture has thickened.
2. Mix in the artichoke hearts, red bell pepper, nutritional yeast, vegan butter, and seasonings, along with salt and pepper.
3. Continue cooking the grits for a further ten to fifteen minutes, stirring them regularly or until they reach a creamy consistency.
4. Green onions that have been chopped should be used as a garnish.

229. LOUISIANA LEMON HERB TOFU

Total Time: 40 minutes

Prep Time: 15 minutes

Ingredients:

- 1 block extra-firm tofu, pressed and cubed
- 2 tablespoons olive oil
- 2 tablespoons Cajun seasoning
- 1 tablespoon lemon zest
- 2 tablespoons lemon juice
- 1 teaspoon dried thyme
- 1 teaspoon garlic powder
- Salt and pepper to taste
- Fresh parsley for garnish

Directions:

1. Cook until the temperature reaches 400 degrees Fahrenheit (200 degrees Celsius).
2. Olive oil, Cajun spice, lemon zest, lemon juice, thyme, garlic powder, salt, and pepper should be mixed together in a bowl along with those ingredients.
3. After adding the tofu cubes to the marinade, mix them again to coat them evenly.
4. After placing the tofu on a baking sheet that has been lined, bake it for twenty-five to thirty minutes, flipping it over halfway through the cooking process.
5. Immediately prior to serving, garnish with fresh parsley.

230. DIRTY CAULIFLOWER RICE

Total Time: 30 minutes

Prep Time: 10 minutes

Ingredients:

- 1 head cauliflower, grated
- 2 tablespoons vegetable oil
- 1 onion, finely chopped
- 2 bell peppers, diced
- 3 cloves garlic, minced
- 1 cup diced tomatoes
- 1 tablespoon Cajun seasoning
- 1/2 teaspoon smoked paprika
- Salt and pepper to taste
- Green onions for garnish

Directions:

1. Use a food processor to grind the cauliflower until it resembles rice, and then set it aside when the processing is complete.
2. A large saucepan over medium heat should be used to get the vegetable oil to the required temperature. The garlic, onions, and bell peppers should be added. To soften, continue cooking.
3. Incorporate chopped tomatoes, Cajun spice, smoked paprika, salt, and pepper into the mixture. Also include cauliflower rice. Bake for ten to twelve minutes, stirring the mixture regularly.
4. Prior to serving, garnish with green onions that have been chopped.

231. VEGAN CAJUN MAC AND CHEESE

Total Time: 45 minutes

Prep Time: 15 minutes

Ingredients:

- 2 cups elbow macaroni, cooked according to package instructions
- 1 cup raw cashews, soaked in hot water for 1 hour
- 1 cup unsweetened almond milk
- 1/4 cup nutritional yeast

- 2 tablespoons lemon juice
- 1 teaspoon Dijon mustard
- 1 teaspoon Cajun seasoning
- 1/2 teaspoon garlic powder
- Salt and pepper to taste
- Chopped chives for garnish

Directions:

1. Cashews that have been soaked, almond milk, nutritional yeast, lemon juice, Dijon mustard, Cajun spice, garlic powder, salt, and pepper should be the ingredients that are blended together in a blender. Blend until it is completely smooth.
2. Prepare the macaroni in accordance with the directions in the box.
3. Place the macaroni in a bowl and add the sauce that has been cooked.
4. To finish, sprinkle some chopped chives on top before serving.

232. CAJUN QUINOA CAKES

Total Time: 50 minutes

Prep Time: 20 minutes

Ingredients:

- 1 cup quinoa, cooked and cooled
- 1 cup black beans, mashed
- 1/2 cup breadcrumbs
- 1/4 cup finely chopped bell peppers
- 2 tablespoons Cajun seasoning
- 1 tablespoon flaxseed meal mixed with 3 tablespoons water (flax egg)
- 2 tablespoons olive oil
- Salt and pepper to taste
- Lemon wedges for serving

Directions:

1. All of the following ingredients should be mixed together in a big bowl: quinoa, mashed black beans, breadcrumbs, bell peppers, Cajun spice, flax egg, salt, and pepper.
2. The ingredients should be formed into patties.
3. Gather the olive oil and heat it in a skillet over medium heat.
4. In order to get a golden brown color, cook the quinoa cakes for three to four minutes on each side.
5. It is recommended to serve lemon wedges on the side.

233. VEGAN DIRTY RICE-STUFFED ZUCCHINI

Total Time: 1 hour

Prep Time: 30 minutes

Ingredients:

- 4 medium zucchinis
- 1 cup brown rice, cooked
- 1 cup vegan ground meat substitute
- 1 onion, finely chopped
- 1 bell pepper, diced
- 2 celery stalks, finely chopped
- 3 cloves garlic, minced
- 1 teaspoon Cajun seasoning
- 1 teaspoon paprika
- 1/2 teaspoon thyme
- Salt and pepper to taste
- 2 cups tomato sauce

Directions:

1. Cook until the oven reaches a temperature of 375 degrees Fahrenheit (190 degrees Celsius).
2. The zucchini should be cut in half lengthwise, and the core should be scooped out, leaving behind a structure that resembles a boat.
3. Sauté the onion, bell pepper, celery, and garlic in a large pan until the vegetables have become more tender.
4. Cajun spice, paprika, thyme, salt, and pepper should be added to the vegan ground beef replacement prior to cooking. Cook the meat replacement until it has a browned appearance.
5. The tomato sauce and the rice that has been cooked should be combined well.
6. Wait an extra five minutes before serving.
7. Prepare a baking dish and fill each zucchini boat with the rice mixture. Place the boats in the dish.
8. Bake for thirty minutes while covered with aluminum foil. Continue baking for a further ten minutes after removing the cover, until the zucchinis are soft.

234.   CREOLE-STYLE STUFFED BELL PEPPER SOUP

Total Time: 1 hour

Prep Time: 20 minutes

Ingredients:

- 1 cup quinoa, rinsed
- 4 bell peppers, diced
- 1 onion, finely chopped
- 3 cloves garlic, minced
- 1 can (15 oz) black beans, drained and rinsed
- 1 can (15 oz) diced tomatoes

- 4 cups vegetable broth
- 2 teaspoons Creole seasoning
- 1 teaspoon thyme
- Salt and pepper to taste
- 1 cup okra, sliced (optional)
- Chopped green onions for garnish

Directions:

1. Onion and garlic should be sautéed in a big saucepan until they get aromatic.
2. Creole spice, thyme, salt, and pepper should be added to the mixture, along with diced tomatoes, diced bell peppers, quinoa, black beans, and diced tomatoes.
3. The heat should be reduced when the mixture has reached a boil, and it should be allowed to simmer for another thirty minutes.
4. If you are using sliced okra, add that now and continue to boil for another ten minutes.
5. Green onions that have been chopped should be used as a garnish.

235. VEGAN ANDOUILLE SAUSAGE GUMBO

Total Time: 1 hour and 30 minutes

Prep Time: 40 minutes

Ingredients:

- 1 cup okra, sliced
- 1 cup vegan Andouille sausage, sliced
- 1 onion, finely chopped
- 1 bell pepper, diced
- 3 celery stalks, finely chopped
- 4 cloves garlic, minced
- 1/2 cup flour
- 1/2 cup vegetable oil
- 4 cups vegetable broth
- 1 can (15 oz) diced tomatoes
- 2 teaspoons Cajun seasoning
- 1 teaspoon thyme
- Salt and pepper to taste
- 3 cups cooked rice

Directions:

1. Flour and vegetable oil should be mixed together in a large pot and whisked together over medium heat until the mixture reaches a dark brown color. This will make a roux.
2. Include garlic, onion, bell pepper, and celery in the mixture. To ensure that the veggies are cooked through.
3. Incorporate the okra, vegan Andouille sausage, diced tomatoes, Cajun spice, thyme, salt, and pepper into the mixture. Stir until everything is well distributed.
4. Simmer for forty-five to sixty minutes or until the flavors have merged.
5. While the rice is cooking, serve.

236. VEGAN CORNBREAD MUFFINS

Total Time: 30 minutes

Prep Time: 10 minutes

Ingredients:

- 1 cup cornmeal
- 1 cup all-purpose flour
- 1 tablespoon baking powder
- 1/2 teaspoon salt
- 1 cup non-dairy milk
- 1/4 cup vegetable oil
- 1/4 cup maple syrup

Directions:

1. Cook until the temperature reaches 400 degrees Fahrenheit (200 degrees Celsius). A muffin tray should be greased or lined.
2. The cornmeal, flour, baking powder, and salt should be mixed together in a large basin using a whisk.
3. Place the non-dairy milk, vegetable oil, and maple syrup in a separate bowl and mix them together.
4. To the dry ingredients add the wet components and whisk until the ingredients are almost completely blended.
5. Mound the mixture about two-thirds of the way into each muffin pan.
6. Bake for fifteen to twenty minutes or until a toothpick comes out clean when put into the center of the cake.

237.   SPICY VEGAN GRITS CAKES

Total Time: 45 minutes

Prep Time: 15 minutes

Ingredients:

- 1 cup grits
- 3 cups water
- 1 cup almond milk
- 1/2 cup nutritional yeast
- 1/4 cup vegan butter

- 1 tsp Cajun seasoning
- 1/2 tsp garlic powder
- Salt and pepper to taste
- Cooking spray

Directions:

1. The water and almond milk should be brought to a boil in a pot, and the mixture should be stirred occasionally. The grits should be stirred in after the pan has been removed from the heat. Make sure to stir the mixture often while it is cooking.
2. Cajun spice, nutritional yeast, vegan butter, garlic powder, salt, and pepper should be added to the mixture. Combine thoroughly.
3. Refrigerate the mixture until it becomes firm, then pour it into a baking dish that has been buttered.
4. Get the oven hot, about 190 degrees Celsius (375 degrees Fahrenheit). Place the cooled grits on a baking sheet and cut them into cakes.
5. Cook for twenty-five to thirty minutes or until the edges are a golden brown color. Serve when still heated.

238. VEGETARIAN HUSHPUPPIES TOPPED WITH REMOULADE

Total Time: 30 minutes

Prep Time: 15 minutes

Ingredients:

- 1 cup cornmeal
- 1/2 cup flour
- 1 tsp baking powder
- 1/2 tsp baking soda
- 1/2 cup onion, finely chopped
- 1/4 cup green bell pepper, finely chopped
- 1/4 cup celery, finely chopped
- 1 cup almond milk
- 2 tbsp flaxseed meal mixed with 6 tbsp water (flax egg)
- Oil for frying

Directions:

1. A bowl should be used to combine cornmeal, flour, baking powder, and baking soda. Bring the batter to a boil.
2. All of the following ingredients should be added to the mixture: almond milk, flax egg, onion, green bell pepper, and celery. Maintain the mixing process until everything is completely combined.
3. At the beginning of the frying process, use a large saucepan or deep fryer to get the oil to a temperature of 175 degrees Celsius (350 degrees Fahrenheit). Maintain this temperature throughout the cooking process.
4. Place heaping spoonfuls of batter into the oil that has been heated, and allow it to fry for around three to four minutes or until it reaches a golden brown color.
5. Utilizing a slotted spoon, remove the hushpuppies and place them on paper towels to drain. Include vegan remoulade on the table.

239.　CREOLE ROASTED EGGPLANT

Total Time: 40 minutes

Prep Time: 15 minutes

Ingredients:

- 2 large eggplants, sliced
- 1/4 cup olive oil
- 2 tbsp Cajun seasoning
- 1 tsp smoked paprika
- 1 tsp dried thyme
- Salt and pepper to taste
- Fresh parsley for garnish

Directions:

1. Roast the vegetables until they are soft, about 20 minutes before serving. The eggplant slices should be placed on a baking pan.
2. Olive oil, Cajun spice, smoked paprika, thyme, salt, and pepper should be combined in a small bowl and shaken together.
3. Application of the oil mixture on both sides of the eggplant slices is recommended.
4. In the oven, roast for twenty-five to thirty minutes, turning once halfway through, until the meat is golden brown and tender.
5. Immediately prior to serving, garnish with fresh parsley.

240. VEGAN RED BEAN DIP

Total Time: 15 minutes

Prep Time: 10 minutes

Ingredients:

- 1 can (15 oz) red beans, drained and rinsed
- 2 cloves garlic, minced
- 1/4 cup tahini
- 2 tbsp lemon juice
- 1 tsp Cajun seasoning
- Salt and pepper to taste
- Olive oil for drizzling
- Chopped green onions for garnish

Directions:

1. Combine the red beans, garlic, tahini, lemon juice, and Cajun spice in a food processor. Process until just combined. Blend until it is completely smooth.
2. Add pepper and salt to taste, and season with salt when you are done.
3. If the consistency is too thick, add more water to adjust it.
4. After transferring to a serving plate, sprinkle with olive oil and garnish with green onions that have been chopped (optional).
5. Pita chips or veggie sticks should be served alongside.

241.   VEGAN DIRTY RICE-STUFFED BELL PEPPERS

Total Time: 1 hour 30 minutes

Prep Time: 30 minutes

Ingredients:

- 4 large bell peppers, halved and cleaned
- 1 cup brown rice, cooked
- 1 cup vegan sausage, crumbled
- 1 onion, finely chopped
- 2 celery stalks, diced
- 1 bell pepper, diced
- 3 cloves garlic, minced
- 1 can (15 oz) diced tomatoes
- 1 cup vegetable broth
- 1 tablespoon Cajun seasoning
- Salt and pepper to taste
- Fresh parsley for garnish

Directions:

1. Get the oven hot, about 190 degrees Celsius (375 degrees Fahrenheit).
2. Sauté the onion, celery, bell pepper, and garlic in a large pan until the vegetables have become more tender.
3. When it is browned, add crumbled vegan sausage and continue to cook.
4. Incorporate the rice that has been cooked, diced tomatoes, vegetable broth, Cajun spice, salt, and pepper into the mixture. Let it simmer for ten minutes.
5. Before putting the bell pepper halves in the oven, load them with the rice mixture and place them on a baking dish.
6. Bake the peppers for forty to forty-five minutes or until they are soft.
7. Immediately prior to serving, garnish with fresh parsley.

242. VEGAN GUMBO BURGER

Total Time: 45 minutes

Prep Time: 15 minutes

Ingredients:

- 1 can (15 oz) black beans, drained and rinsed
- 1 cup okra, chopped
- 1/2 cup bell pepper, finely chopped
- 1/4 cup onion, minced
- 2 cloves garlic, minced
- 1 cup breadcrumbs
- 1 tablespoon Cajun seasoning
- Salt and pepper to taste
- Burger buns
- Vegan mayo, lettuce, and tomato for toppings

Directions:

1. You may use a potato masher or a fork to mash the black beans that are in a bowl.
2. Incorporate the following *Ingredients:* breadcrumbs, Cajun spice, chopped okra, bell pepper, onion, garlic, and salt & pepper after thoroughly combining, mix.
3. Burger patties should be formed from the ingredients.
4. Cook the patties on each side for four to five minutes in a pan that has been heated over medium heat.
5. The burger buns should be toasted before being assembled with vegan mayonnaise, lettuce, and tomato.

243.   RED BEANS AND QUINOA

Total Time: 40 minutes

Prep Time: 15 minutes

Ingredients:

- 1 cup quinoa, rinsed
- 2 cups cooked red beans
- 1 onion, diced
- 2 cloves garlic, minced
- 1 bell pepper, diced
- 1 celery stalk, diced

- 1 can (15 oz) diced tomatoes
- 2 cups vegetable broth
- 1 tablespoon Cajun seasoning
- Salt and pepper to taste
- Green onions for garnish

Directions:

1. The onion, garlic, bell pepper, and celery should be sautéed in a saucepan until they become more tender.
2. Mix in some Cajun seasoning, some salt, some pepper, some chopped tomatoes, some diced quinoa, and some diced red beans. Allow to come to a simmer.
3. The quinoa should be cooked, and the liquid should be absorbed after twenty minutes of cooking with the lid on.
4. Prior to serving, garnish with green onions that have been chopped.

244. DIRTY RICE-STUFFED PATTYPAN SQUASH TACOS

Total Time: 1 hour

Prep Time: 30 minutes

Ingredients:

- 8 pattypan squash, halved and scooped
- 1 cup white rice, cooked
- 1 cup vegan ground meat
- 1 onion, finely chopped
- 1 bell pepper, diced
- 2 cloves garlic, minced

- 1 can (15 oz) black beans, drained and rinsed
- 1 tablespoon Cajun seasoning
- Salt and pepper to taste
- Taco shells
- Avocado, salsa, and cilantro for toppings

Directions:

1. Get the oven hot, about 190 degrees Celsius (375 degrees Fahrenheit).
2. Pattypan squash halves should be boiled or steamed until they are subtly soft. Create a cavity by sucking out the middle of the object.
3. To soften the onion, bell pepper, and garlic, sauté them in a pan until they are tender.
4. Cajun seasoning, black beans, cooked rice, vegan ground beef, and salt and pepper should be added to the mixture. Continue to cook until the food is completely heated.
5. Place the pattypan squash halves in a baking dish after stuffing them with the rice mixture and placing them in the dish.
6. Bake for twenty-five to twenty-five minutes.
7. Taco shells should be used to serve the filled squash, and avocado, salsa, and cilantro should be placed on top.

245.   CREOLE-STYLE LENTIL LOAF

Total Time: 1 hour 30 minutes

Prep Time: 20 minutes

Ingredients:

- 2 cups cooked green lentils
- 1 cup breadcrumbs
- 1 onion, finely chopped
- 1 bell pepper, diced
- 2 celery stalks, finely chopped
- 3 cloves garlic, minced
- 1 tablespoon Cajun seasoning
- 1 teaspoon thyme
- 1 teaspoon paprika
- 1/2 cup tomato sauce
- 2 tablespoons flaxseed meal mixed with 6 tablespoons water (flax egg)
- Salt and pepper to taste

Directions:

1. Bring the temperature of the oven up to 175 degrees Celsius (350 degrees Fahrenheit).
2. Lentils that have been cooked, breadcrumbs, onion, bell pepper, celery, garlic, Cajun spice, thyme, paprika, tomato sauce, and flax egg should be mixed together in a big bowl containing all of the ingredients. Combine thoroughly.
3. Add pepper and salt to taste, and season with salt when you are done.
4. The ingredients should be shaped into a loaf and then transferred onto a loaf pan that has been oiled.
5. For one hour, or until the top is a golden brown color, bake the dish.
6. If you want to slice the lentil loaf, you need to wait ten minutes for it to cool down.
7. Serve the slices with the Cajun-inspired sides that you enjoy the most.

246.   CREOLE LENTIL STEW

Total Time: 45 minutes

Prep Time: 15 minutes

Ingredients:

- 1 cup dry green or brown lentils
- 1 onion, diced
- 2 bell peppers, chopped
- 3 celery stalks, sliced
- 3 cloves garlic, minced
- 1 can diced tomatoes
- 4 cups vegetable broth
- 1 tablespoon Cajun seasoning
- 1 teaspoon thyme
- 1 bay leaf
- Salt and pepper to taste
- Green onions for garnish

Directions:

1. After rinsing, leave the lentils aside.
2. Sauté the onion, bell peppers, celery, and garlic in a large saucepan until the vegetables have become more tender.
3. The lentils, chopped tomatoes, vegetable broth, Cajun spice, thyme, bay leaf, salt, and pepper should be added to the ingredients.
4. If the lentils aren't cooked after 30–35 minutes of simmering, reduce heat to low and simmer for another 30–35 minutes.
5. Get rid of the bay leaf before you serve.
6. A garnish of chopped green onions is recommended, and the dish can be served on crusty bread or over rice.

247.   SWEET POTATO AND LENTIL GUMBO BOWLS

Total Time: 1 hour

Prep Time: 20 minutes

Ingredients:

- 2 sweet potatoes, diced
- 1 cup dry green or brown lentils
- 1 onion, finely chopped
- 3 cloves garlic, minced
- 1 bell pepper, sliced
- 3 celery stalks, chopped
- 1 can okra, drained
- 1 can diced tomatoes
- 4 cups vegetable broth
- 2 tablespoons Cajun seasoning
- 1 teaspoon thyme
- Salt and pepper to taste
- Cooked rice for serving

Directions:

1. Sauté the onion, garlic, bell pepper, and celery in a large saucepan until the vegetables have become more tender.
2. Cajun seasoning, thyme, salt, and pepper should be added to the mixture, along with sweet potatoes, lentils, okra, chopped tomatoes, and vegetable broth.
3. After coming to a boil, simmer the lentils and sweet potatoes for 40–45 minutes to cook.
4. The dish should be served over cooked rice and topped with fresh thyme.

248. SWEET POTATO AND CHICKPEA GRITS TACOS

Total Time: 40 minutes

Prep Time: 20 minutes

Ingredients:

- 2 sweet potatoes, peeled and cubed
- 1 can chickpeas, drained and rinsed
- 1 cup stone-ground grits
- 4 cups vegetable broth
- 1 teaspoon smoked paprika
- 1 teaspoon cumin
- Salt and pepper to taste
- Corn tortillas
- Avocado slices, salsa, and cilantro for topping

Directions:

1. Let sweet potatoes boil until they are soft. Drain, then keep away for later use.
2. To prepare the vegetable broth, bring it to a boil in a separate saucepan. Include smoked paprika, cumin, smoked paprika, grits, salt, and pepper. Cook in accordance with the instructions on the box.
3. Chickpeas and sweet potatoes that have been cooked should be sautéed in a pan until they are gently browned.
4. The tacos should be assembled with grits, chickpeas, and sweet potato combinations, and corn tortillas should be warmed.
5. Avocado slices, salsa, and cilantro should be sprinkled on top.
6. Serve as soon as possible.

249. CAJUN QUINOA-STUFFED ZUCCHINI BOATS

Total Time: 40 minutes

Prep Time: 15 minutes

Ingredients:

- 4 medium-sized zucchini
- 1 cup quinoa, cooked
- 1 can (15 oz) black beans, drained and rinsed
- 1 cup corn kernels
- 1 cup cherry tomatoes, diced
- 1/2 cup red onion, finely chopped

- 2 cloves garlic, minced
- 1 teaspoon Cajun seasoning
- Salt and pepper to taste
- 1/4 cup fresh cilantro, chopped (for garnish)
- 2 tablespoons olive oil

Directions:

1. Get the oven hot, about 190 degrees Celsius (375 degrees Fahrenheit).
2. Remove the seeds from the zucchini by cutting them in half lengthwise and scooping them out to make boats.
3. Combine the quinoa that has been cooked, the black beans, the corn, the cherry tomatoes, the red onion, the garlic, the Cajun spice, the salt, and the pepper in a large bowl. Combine thoroughly.
4. The zucchini boats should be placed on a baking sheet, and the quinoa mixture should be stuffed into each boat.
5. Pour olive oil over the top, then bake for twenty-five to thirty minutes or until the zucchini is soft, whichever comes first.
6. Fresh cilantro should be used as a garnish before serving.

250. VEGAN RED PEPPER BISQUE

Total Time: 45 minutes

Prep Time: 15 minutes

Ingredients:

- 3 red bell peppers, roasted and peeled
- 1 onion, diced
- 2 cloves garlic, minced
- 1 can (28 oz) crushed tomatoes
- 4 cups vegetable broth
- 1 cup coconut milk
- 2 tablespoons olive oil
- 1 teaspoon Cajun seasoning
- Salt and pepper to taste
- Fresh basil leaves for garnish

Directions:

1. To soften the onion and garlic, sauté them in olive oil in a big saucepan until they are tender.
2. Roasted red peppers, crushed tomatoes, vegetable broth, coconut milk, Cajun spice, freshly ground black pepper, and salt should be added. Assume a boiling point.
3. Simmer for twenty to twenty-five minutes; reduce the heat.
4. To get a smooth consistency, purée the soup using an immersion blender.
5. Before serving hot, taste and adjust spice as needed. Top with fresh basil.

251. ZESTY CABBAGE AND BLACK BEAN SOUP

Total Time: 1 hour

Prep Time: 20 minutes

Ingredients:

- 1 small green cabbage, shredded
- 1 can (15 oz) black beans, drained and rinsed
- 1 onion, chopped
- 2 carrots, diced
- 3 cloves garlic, minced
- 1 can (28 oz) diced tomatoes
- 6 cups vegetable broth
- 1 teaspoon Cajun seasoning
- 1 teaspoon paprika
- Salt and pepper to taste
- Fresh parsley for garnish

Directions:

1. To soften the onion, carrots, and garlic, sauté them in a large saucepan until they are tender.
2. Paprika, Cajun flavor, shredded cabbage, black beans, diced tomatoes, vegetable broth, and salt and pepper are the ingredients that should be included. Assume a boiling point.
3. Maintain a low simmer for forty to forty-five minutes.
4. Make any necessary adjustments to the seasoning, and serve the dish hot, garnished with fresh parsley.

252. SPICY CREOLE BRUSSELS SPROUTS

Total Time: 30 minutes

Prep Time: 10 minutes

Ingredients:

- 1 lb Brussels sprouts, trimmed and halved
- 2 tablespoons olive oil
- 1 tablespoon Cajun seasoning
- 1 teaspoon smoked paprika
- 1/2 teaspoon garlic powder
- Salt and pepper to taste
- Lemon wedges for serving

Directions:

1. Roast the vegetables until they are soft, about 20 minutes before serving.
2. Brussels sprouts should be tossed in olive oil, Cajun spice, smoked paprika, garlic powder, salt, and pepper in a dish containing the Brussels sprouts.
3. Position the Brussels sprouts in a single layer on a baking sheet and set it in the oven.
4. Bake for twenty to twenty-five minutes or until the surface is brown and crispy.
5. Serve while still hot, with slices of lemon on the side.

253.   VEGAN BISCUITS WITH CREOLE GRAVY

Total Time: 35 minutes

Prep Time: 15 minutes

Cook Time: 20 minutes

Ingredients:

- 2 cups all-purpose flour
- 1 tablespoon baking powder
- 1/2 teaspoon baking soda
- 1/2 teaspoon salt
- 1 cup almond milk (or any plant-based milk)
- 1 tablespoon apple cider vinegar
- 1/3 cup coconut oil, solid
- 1 tablespoon maple syrup

- For the Creole Gravy:
- 2 tablespoons vegan butter
- 1/4 cup all-purpose flour
- 1 cup vegetable broth
- 1 cup unsweetened almond milk
- 1 teaspoon Creole seasoning
- 1/2 teaspoon garlic powder
- Salt and pepper to taste

Directions:

1. Set a parchment-lined baking sheet in a preheated oven set to 425 degrees Fahrenheit (220 degrees Celsius).
2. Both the almond milk and the apple cider vinegar should be mixed together in a small basin. The vegan buttermilk may be made by allowing it to settle for five minutes.
3. It is best to use a big mixing bowl and a whisk-free method to combine the flour, baking powder, baking soda, and salt.
4. Use a pastry cutter or your hands to combine the dry ingredients with the solid coconut oil until the mixture resembles coarse crumbs.
5. Use the pastry cutter to incorporate the oil.
6. Include the combination of almond milk and maple syrup in the mixture. While taking caution not to overmix, stir the ingredients until they are almost completely incorporated.
7. Flip the dough out onto a surface that has been dusted with flour. Form it into a rectangle with a thickness of one inch. Make biscuits by cutting them out using a biscuit cutter and placing them on the baking sheet that has been prepared.

8. Place the biscuits in the oven and bake for 12 to 15 minutes or until the tops are golden brown.
9. As the biscuits are baking, you should get started on making the Creole gravy. To melt the vegan butter, place it in a pot and heat it around medium. After stirring in the flour to make a roux, continue cooking for one to two minutes.
10. The vegetable broth and almond milk should be whisked in gradually until the mixture is smooth. Now is the time to add the garlic powder, salt, pepper, and Creole spice. Simmer for five to seven minutes or until the gravy has reached the desired consistency.
11. When you are finished cooking the biscuits, serve them while they are still warm with a large amount of Creole gravy on top. Take pleasure in your vegan biscuits topped with creole gravy.

254. VEGAN JAMBALAYA DELIGHT

Total Time: 45 minutes

Prep Time: 15 minutes

Ingredients:

- 2 cups long-grain white rice
- 1 tablespoon vegetable oil
- 1 onion, diced
- 1 bell pepper, diced
- 2 celery stalks, diced
- 3 cloves garlic, minced
- 1 can (14 oz) diced tomatoes, undrained
- 1 cup vegetable broth
- 1 teaspoon smoked paprika
- 1 teaspoon thyme
- 1 teaspoon oregano
- 1/2 teaspoon cayenne pepper
- Salt and pepper to taste
- 1 cup vegan sausage, sliced
- 1 cup okra, sliced
- 1 cup kidney beans, cooked

Directions:

1. Prepare the rice in accordance with the directions on the package.
2. Prepare the oil by heating it in a big saucepan over medium heat. Include the celery, onion, and bell pepper in the dish. To soften the meat, sauté it.
3. Garlic should be added and sautéed for one more minute.

4. Combine chopped tomatoes, vegetable broth, smoked paprika, thyme, oregano, cayenne pepper, salt, and pepper. Stir until everything is evenly distributed. Allow to come to a simmer.
5. Include kidney beans, okra, and vegan sausage in the dish. For fifteen to twenty minutes, whisk the mixture occasionally.
6. Over rice that has been cooked, serve the jambalaya.

255. VEGAN BOUDIN SAUSAGE ROLLS

Total Time: 1 hour

Prep Time: 30 minutes

Ingredients:

- 1 pound vegan boudin sausage
- 1 sheet vegan puff pastry, thawed
- 1 tablespoon Dijon mustard
- 1 tablespoon maple syrup
- 1 tablespoon olive oil

Directions:

1. Get the oven hot, about 190 degrees Celsius (375 degrees Fahrenheit).
2. Put the sheet of puff pastry on a surface that has been dusted with flour.
3. Distribute the mustard made from Dijon over the pastry sheet.
4. Take off the casing from the vegan boudin sausage, and then position the filling in the middle of the pastry.
5. Using a rolling pin, tightly wrap the pastry around the filling and then seal the edges.
6. The roll should be placed on a baking pan. The roll should be brushed with the combination that was made by combining maple syrup and olive oil.
7. Cook for thirty to thirty-five minutes or until the pastry has a golden brown color.
8. Wait a few minutes before slicing it and serving it to allow it to cool down.

256. VEGAN DIRTY RICE WITH TOFURKY SAUSAGE

Total Time: 50 minutes

Prep Time: 20 minutes

Ingredients:

- 1 cup brown rice
- 2 cups vegetable broth
- 1 tablespoon vegetable oil
- 1 onion, finely chopped
- 1 bell pepper, finely chopped
- 2 celery stalks, finely chopped
- 3 cloves garlic, minced

- 1 package (14 oz) Tofurky sausage, crumbled
- 1 teaspoon paprika
- 1 teaspoon dried thyme
- 1/2 teaspoon cayenne pepper
- Salt and pepper to taste
- Green onions for garnish

Directions:

1. Follow the package directions to a tee while cooking the brown rice in vegetable broth.
2. Simmer the oil in a large pan over medium heat.
3. Include garlic, onion, bell pepper, and celery in the mixture. Sauté the veggies until they become tender.
4. For a browned appearance, add crumbled Tofurky sausage to the skillet and continue to cook it.
5. Paprika, thyme, cayenne pepper, salt, and pepper should be stirred in the mixture.
6. Mix the rice that has been cooked thoroughly in the skillet.
7. Add another five to ten minutes of cooking time until the flavors have merged.
8. Prior to serving, garnish with green onions that have been chopped.

257. CREOLE STUFFED BELL PEPPER TACOS

Total Time: 40 minutes

Prep Time: 20 minutes

Ingredients:

- 4 large bell peppers, halved and seeds removed
- 1 cup cooked white rice
- 1 cup black beans, drained and rinsed
- 1 cup corn kernels
- 1 cup diced tomatoes
- 1 cup diced red onion
- 1 cup diced zucchini
- 1 tablespoon Creole seasoning
- 1 teaspoon garlic powder
- Salt and pepper to taste
- 1 cup shredded vegan cheese
- 8 small taco shells
- Fresh cilantro for garnish

Directions:

1. Get the oven hot, about 190 degrees Celsius (375 degrees Fahrenheit).
2. Put everything in a big basin and stir:
3. Rice that has been cooked, black beans, corn, tomatoes, red onion, zucchini, Creole seasoning, garlic powder, salt, and pepper according to taste. Combine thoroughly.
4. Place a portion of the rice and veggie mixture inside of each half of the bell pepper.
5. After packing the peppers, place them in a baking dish and cover with foil.
6. Take the dish out of the oven and bake it for twenty minutes. After that, remove the foil, sprinkle vegan cheese on top, and continue baking for another ten minutes or until the cheese is melted and bubbling.
7. Preheating the taco shells in accordance with the instructions on the box should be done while the peppers are baking.
8. Whenever the peppers are ready, you may put together the tacos by stuffing each taco shell with a pepper that has been filled.
9. You should serve it hot and garnish it with fresh cilantro.

258. VEGAN MARDI GRAS CUPCAKES

Total Time: 1 hour

Prep Time: 20 minutes

Ingredients:

- 2 cups all-purpose flour
- 1 cup granulated sugar
- 1 teaspoon baking soda
- 1/2 teaspoon salt
- 1 cup almond milk
- 1/2 cup vegetable oil

- 2 tablespoons white vinegar
- 1 teaspoon vanilla extract
- Purple, green, and yellow vegan food coloring
- Vegan cream cheese frosting
- Mardi Gras-themed sprinkles

Directions:

1. Before you line a cupcake pan with paper liners and grease it, get your oven preheated to 350 degrees Fahrenheit (175 degrees Celsius).
2. Utilizing a whisk, combine the flour, sugar, baking soda, and salt in a sizable basin.
3. Put the almond milk, vegetable oil, white vinegar, and vanilla essence in their own bowl or container and mix them together.
4. A thorough blending of the dry and wet components should be achieved by combining them together.
5. Put the batter into three equal sections and divide it further.
6. In order to get the required hue, add food coloring purple to one portion, green to another piece, and yellow to the third portion. Mix each color until it reaches the desired level.
7. It is possible to create layered effects by spooning a small amount of each colored batter into each cupcake liner.
8. Cook for twenty-five to twenty-five minutes, or until a toothpick inserted into the middle of the cake comes out clean.
9. You should wait until the cupcakes have completely cooled down before icing them with vegan cream cheese frosting and topping them with sprinkles that have a Mardi Gras theme.

259. DIRTY RICE-STUFFED BELL PEPPER SOUP

Total Time: 1 hour

Prep Time: 30 minutes

Ingredients:

- 4 bell peppers, diced
- 1 cup celery, diced
- 1 cup onion, diced
- 1 cup vegan sausage, crumbled
- 2 cups cooked brown rice
- 4 cups vegetable broth
- 1 can (14 oz) diced tomatoes
- 1 teaspoon Cajun seasoning
- 1/2 teaspoon thyme
- Salt and pepper to taste
- Fresh parsley for garnish

Directions:

1. Bell peppers, celery, and onion should be sautéed in a big saucepan until they become more tender.
2. When it is browned, add crumbled vegan sausage and continue to cook.
3. Cajun spice, thyme, salt, and pepper should be stirred in together with cooked brown rice, vegetable broth, chopped tomatoes, and Cajun seasoning.
4. To prepare the soup, bring it to a boil, then decrease the heat and let it simmer for half an hour.
5. After adjusting the ingredients to your liking, serve the dish hot, garnished with fresh parsley.

260. VEGAN GUMBO PIZZA

Total Time: 45 minutes

Prep Time: 15 minutes

Ingredients:

- 1 pre-made pizza crust
- 1 cup okra, sliced
- 1 cup bell peppers, thinly sliced
- 1 cup vegan andouille sausage, sliced
- 1 cup diced tomatoes
- 1 cup vegan mozzarella cheese, shredded

- 1/4 cup tomato sauce
- 1 tablespoon Cajun seasoning
- 1 teaspoon dried thyme
- 1 teaspoon garlic powder
- Hot sauce to taste
- Fresh parsley for garnish

Directions:

1. To prepare the pizza dough, preheat the oven to the temperature that is stated on the package.
2. Cook the okra, bell peppers, and vegan andouille sausage in a pan until the vegetables are just beginning to get soft.
3. The pizza dough should be covered with tomato sauce in a uniform layer.
4. The sauce should be seasoned with Cajun spice, dried thyme, and garlic powder before it is served.
5. Make a layer of sausage and veggies that have been sautéed on top of the sauce.
6. Include vegan mozzarella cheese and chopped tomatoes in the mixture.
7. Bake or bake until the crust is golden brown and the cheese is melted, whichever comes first, according to the instructions on the pizza dough packaging.
8. Before serving, drizzle spicy sauce over the pizza and top it with fresh parsley as a garnish if desired.

261.   SPICY CAJUN QUINOA BOWL

Total Time: 30 minutes

Prep Time: 15 minutes

Servings: 4

Ingredients:

- 1 cup quinoa, rinsed
- 2 cups vegetable broth
- 1 tablespoon olive oil
- 1 onion, diced
- 2 bell peppers, diced
- 1 cup cherry tomatoes, halved
- 1 can black beans, drained and rinsed
- 1 teaspoon Cajun seasoning
- 1/2 teaspoon smoked paprika
- Salt and pepper to taste
- Fresh cilantro for garnish

Directions:

1. Quinoa and vegetable broth should be mixed together in a medium-sized pot. The quinoa needs about fifteen minutes to simmer after it comes to a boil, so reduce the heat to low, cover, and keep cooking.
2. Get the olive oil ready by warming it in a large saucepan over medium heat. Sauté the diced onion and bell peppers until they come to a softened state.
3. Salt, pepper, smoked paprika, and Cajun spice should be added to the skillet, along with black beans, cherry tomatoes, and Cajun seasoning. In order to mix, stir.
4. The quinoa should be added to the skillet after it is done, and then everything should be mixed together.
5. To let the flavors combine, continue cooking for an additional five minutes. When necessary, adjust the seasoning.
6. The dish should be served in bowls and topped with fresh cilantro.

262. DIRTY RICE-STUFFED BELL PEPPER SKILLET

Total Time: 45 minutes

Prep Time: 20 minutes

Servings: 6

Ingredients:

- 1 cup brown rice, cooked
- 1 tablespoon olive oil
- 1 onion, finely chopped
- 2 celery stalks, diced
- 1 bell pepper, diced
- 1 cup vegan sausage, crumbled
- 1 tablespoon Cajun seasoning
- 1/2 teaspoon thyme
- 1/4 teaspoon cayenne pepper
- Salt and pepper to taste
- 6 bell peppers, halved and cleaned
- 1 can diced tomatoes, drained
- Green onions for garnish

Directions:

1. Get the oven hot, about 190 degrees Celsius (375 degrees Fahrenheit).
2. One way to get the olive oil ready is to heat it in a big pan over medium heat.
3. Sauté the onion, celery, and bell pepper until they have gained their softness.
4. Crumbled vegan sausage, Cajun spice, thyme, cayenne pepper, salt, and pepper should be added to the mixture. Ensure that the sausage is browned by cooking it.
5. Mix in the diced tomatoes and brown rice that has been cooked. Combine thoroughly.
6. Place bell peppers that have been cut in half in the skillet, and then pour the rice mixture into each pepper with a spoon.
7. Bake the peppers and cover them with a lid or foil for twenty-five to thirty minutes or until they are soft.
8. Prior to serving, garnish with green onions that have been chopped.

263. VEGAN MARDI GRAS SLAW

Total Time: 20 minutes

Prep Time: 15 minutes

Servings: 8

Ingredients:

- 4 cups shredded cabbage (green and purple mix)
- 1 cup shredded carrots
- 1/2 cup vegan mayonnaise
- 2 tablespoons Dijon mustard
- 1 tablespoon apple cider vinegar
- 1 tablespoon maple syrup
- 1 teaspoon Cajun seasoning
- Salt and pepper to taste
- 1/4 cup chopped fresh parsley

Directions:

1. The shredded cabbage and carrots should be mixed together in a big basin.
2. In a small basin, whisk together vegan mayonnaise, Dijon mustard, maple syrup, apple cider vinegar, Cajun spice, salt, and pepper.
3. Once the dressing has been poured over the cabbage mixture, stir it so it is evenly coated.
4. Place in the refrigerator for at least an hour to enable the flavors to harmonize.
5. Sprinkle some chopped parsley on top of the dish just before serving.

264. SPICY CAJUN COUSCOUS

Total Time: 25 minutes

Prep Time: 10 minutes

Servings: 4

Ingredients:

- 1 cup couscous
- 1 1/4 cups vegetable broth
- 1 tablespoon olive oil
- 1 onion, finely chopped
- 2 cloves garlic, minced
- 1 bell pepper, diced
- 1 zucchini, diced

- 1 can chickpeas, drained and rinsed
- 2 teaspoons Cajun seasoning
- 1/2 teaspoon red pepper flakes (optional)
- Salt and pepper to taste
- Fresh parsley for garnish

Directions:

1. A boil should be reached in a small saucepan containing vegetable broth. Take the skillet off the stove, put the lid on it, and then mix in the couscous. After allowing it to settle for five minutes, fluff it with a fork.
2. One way to get the olive oil ready is to heat it in a big pan over medium heat. Continue to sauté the onion and garlic until they release their aroma.
3. Add chickpeas, bell pepper, and zucchini to the skillet and stir to combine. Allow veggies to cook until they are soft.
4. Include the couscous that has been cooked, Cajun spice, red pepper flakes (if using), salt, and pepper in the mixture. Combine thoroughly.
5. Add an additional three to five minutes of cooking time to enable the flavors to combine.
6. Immediately prior to serving, garnish with fresh parsley.

265. VEGAN BOURBON GLAZED CARROTS

Total Time: 30 minutes

Prep Time: 10 minutes

Ingredients:

- 1 pound baby carrots
- 2 tablespoons olive oil
- 1/4 cup bourbon
- 1/4 cup maple syrup
- 2 tablespoons soy sauce

- 1 teaspoon Dijon mustard
- 1/2 teaspoon garlic powder
- Salt and pepper to taste
- Chopped fresh parsley for garnish (optional)

Directions:

1. Roast the vegetables until they are soft, about 20 minutes before serving.
2. Mix all of the ingredients together in a bowl:
3. Olive oil, bourbon, maple syrup, soy sauce, Dijon mustard, garlic powder, salt, and pepper. Whisk until well combined.
4. On a baking sheet, arrange the baby carrots, and then sprinkle the bourbon mixture over them. Toss the carrots to ensure that they are equally coated.
5. Prepare the carrots by roasting them in the oven for twenty to twenty-five minutes, tossing them halfway through the cooking process.
6. If desired, garnish with chopped parsley. Keep warm and savor the time!

266.   VEGAN BOUDIN-STUFFED BELL PEPPERS

Total Time: 1 hour

Prep Time: 20 minutes

Ingredients:

- 4 large bell peppers, halved and seeds removed
- 1 cup cooked brown rice
- 1 cup cooked lentils
- 1/2 cup diced onions
- 1/2 cup diced celery
- 1/2 cup diced bell peppers (any color)
- 2 cloves garlic, minced
- 1 teaspoon Cajun seasoning
- 1 teaspoon smoked paprika
- Salt and pepper to taste
- 1 cup tomato sauce

Directions:

1. Bring the oven up to a temperature of 375 F (190 C).
2. All of the following ingredients should be mixed together in a big bowl: cooked rice, lentils, chopped onions, celery, bell peppers, garlic, Cajun spice, smoky paprika, salt, and pepper.
3. When you have finished stuffing each half of the bell pepper with the mixture, place them on a baking dish.
4. Over the peppers that have been filled, pour tomato sauce.
5. Wrap the baking dish with aluminum foil and place it in the oven for half an hour. If you want your peppers extra soft, uncover them after 15 minutes and bake them for another 15 or until done.
6. Delight in the Cajun flavors while they are still hot!

267. CAJUN-STYLE VEGAN ETOUFFEE

Total Time: 45 minutes

Prep Time: 15 minutes

Ingredients:

- 1/4 cup vegan butter
- 1/4 cup all-purpose flour
- 1 onion, finely chopped
- 1 bell pepper, diced
- 2 celery stalks, diced
- 3 cloves garlic, minced
- 1 teaspoon Cajun seasoning
- 1/2 teaspoon thyme
- 1 can (14 oz) diced tomatoes
- 1 cup vegetable broth
- 1 pound okra, sliced
- 1 pound vegan sausage, sliced
- Salt and pepper to taste
- Cooked rice for serving

Directions:

1. The vegan butter should be melted in a large pan over medium heat until it is. To make a roux, stir in the flour, then continue to heat it until it reaches a golden brown color.
2. Make sure to include garlic, onions, bell peppers, and celery. Allow veggies to cook until they become tender.
3. Cajun spice, thyme, chopped tomatoes, and vegetable broth should be stirred in at this point. Let it simmer for ten minutes.
4. Cook for a further fifteen minutes after adding sliced okra and vegan sausage to the pot.
5. Before seasoning with salt, add pepper and salt to taste. As the rice cooks, spoon it out.

268. VEGAN BOURBON STREET BBQ TOFU

Total Time: 40 minutes

Prep Time: 15 minutes

Ingredients:

- 1 block extra-firm tofu, pressed and cubed
- 1/2 cup barbecue sauce
- 1/4 cup bourbon
- 2 tablespoons soy sauce
- 1 tablespoon maple syrup
- 1 teaspoon smoked paprika
- 1/2 teaspoon garlic powder
- 1/2 teaspoon onion powder
- 1/4 teaspoon cayenne pepper (optional)
- Green onions, sliced, for garnish

Directions:

1. Bring the oven up to a temperature of 375 F (190 C).
2. To make the barbecue sauce, combine the following ingredients in a bowl: barbecue sauce, bourbon, soy sauce, maple syrup, smoked paprika, garlic powder, onion powder, and cayenne pepper.
3. Be sure to thoroughly cover the cubed tofu in the sauce by tossing it.
4. Bake the tofu for twenty-five to thirty minutes, flipping it over midway through the cooking process, on a baking sheet that has been coated with parchment paper.
5. Add sliced green onions or any desired garnish just before serving. The Vegan Bourbon Street BBQ Tofu is sure to wow your taste buds!

269.   VEGAN BLACKENED VEGGIES

Total Time: 30 minutes

Prep Time: 15 minutes

Ingredients:

- 4 cups mixed vegetables (e.g., bell peppers, zucchini, mushrooms, cherry tomatoes)
- 2 tablespoons olive oil
- 1 tablespoon Cajun seasoning
- 1 teaspoon smoked paprika
- 1 teaspoon garlic powder
- Salt and black pepper to taste
- Lemon wedges for serving

Directions:

1. Roast the vegetables until they are soft, about 20 minutes before serving.
2. Toss the vegetables in a large bowl with the olive oil, Cajun seasoning, smoked paprika, garlic powder, salt, and pepper. Toss to completely coat. Toss until everything is together.
3. A single layer of the veggies that have been seasoned should be spread out on a baking sheet.
4. Roast the vegetables in an oven that has been prepared for fifteen to twenty minutes or until they are soft and have a small blackening around the edges.
5. Take the veggies out of the oven and stir with a little fresh lemon juice just before serving.

270. BLACK BEAN AND CORNBREAD CASSEROLE

Total Time: 1 hour

Prep Time: 20 minutes

Ingredients:

- 2 cans (15 oz each) black beans, drained and rinsed
- 1 cup cornmeal
- 1 cup all-purpose flour
- 1 tablespoon baking powder
- 1 teaspoon salt
- 1 cup non-dairy milk
- 1/4 cup olive oil
- 1 cup corn kernels (fresh or frozen)
- 1 cup diced tomatoes
- 1 cup diced bell peppers
- 1 teaspoon Cajun seasoning

Directions:

1. Bring the oven up to a temperature of 375 F (190 C).
2. Black beans, corn, tomatoes, bell peppers, and Cajun seasoning should be combined in a dish prior to serving. Move to a baking dish and set aside.
3. Cornmeal, flour, baking powder, and salt should be mixed together in a separate large basin. Stir in the olive oil and non-dairy milk until they are almost completely blended.
4. The cornbread batter should be poured over the black bean mixture and spread out in an equal manner.
5. Bake the cornbread in an oven that has been warmed for thirty-five to forty minutes or until it is golden brown and a toothpick inserted into it comes out clean.

271. VEGAN RED BEANS AND QUINOA

Total Time: 45 minutes

Prep Time: 15 minutes

Ingredients:

- 1 cup quinoa, rinsed
- 2 cups cooked red beans
- 1 onion, finely chopped
- 2 celery stalks, chopped
- 1 bell pepper, diced
- 3 cloves garlic, minced

- 1 teaspoon Cajun seasoning
- 1 teaspoon thyme
- 1 bay leaf
- 4 cups vegetable broth
- Salt and black pepper to taste
- Green onions for garnish

Directions:

1. Sauté the onion, celery, and bell pepper in a saucepan until they have become more tender. After adding the garlic, continue to simmer for one more minute.
2. Quinoa, red beans, Cajun spice, thyme, and bay leaf should be stirred in at this point.
3. Put in the veggie broth, bring it to a boil, and then turn the heat down to a low setting. Once the quinoa is done, cover it and let it boil for twenty to twenty-five minutes.
4. Before seasoning with salt, add pepper and salt to taste. Take off the bay leaf before serving.
5. Chopped green onions should be used as a garnish.

272.   VEGAN BAYOU MAC AND CHEESE

Total Time: 40 minutes

Prep Time: 15 minutes

Ingredients:

- 2 cups elbow macaroni (or your favorite pasta)
- 1 cup raw cashews, soaked
- 1 cup peeled and diced potatoes
- 1/2 cup diced carrots
- 1/2 cup nutritional yeast
- 1/4 cup olive oil
- 1 tablespoon lemon juice
- 1 teaspoon garlic powder
- 1 teaspoon onion powder
- 1/2 teaspoon smoked paprika
- Salt and black pepper to taste
- Chopped parsley for garnish

Directions:

1. Make sure to follow the package guidelines while cooking the pasta.
2. Potatoes and carrots should be boiled in a saucepan until they are soft. Drain, then allow to cool off.
3. Cashews that have been soaked, potatoes that have been cooked, carrots, nutritional yeast, olive oil, lemon juice, garlic powder, onion powder, smoked paprika, salt, and pepper should be blended together at a high speed in a blender. Blend until it is completely smooth.
4. Assemble the cheese sauce with the cooked spaghetti until it is completely covered.
5. The Bayou Mac and Cheese should be served hot, with chopped parsley included as a garnish.

273. CREOLE STUFFED PATTYPAN SQUASH

Total Time: 1 hour

Prep Time: 20 minutes

Ingredients:

- 4 medium pattypan squash
- 1 cup cooked quinoa
- 1 can (15 oz) black beans, drained and rinsed
- 1 cup diced tomatoes
- 1/2 cup diced bell peppers (red and green)
- 1/4 cup chopped green onions
- 2 cloves garlic, minced
- 1 teaspoon Cajun seasoning
- Salt and pepper to taste
- 1/4 cup vegan cheese, shredded (optional)
- Fresh parsley for garnish

Directions:

1. Bring the oven up to a temperature of 375 F (190 C).
2. After removing the tips of the pattypan squash, scrape out the seeds to create a hollow within the core of the squash.
3. The quinoa, black beans, tomatoes, bell peppers, green onions, garlic, Cajun spice, salt, and pepper should be mixed together with the individual ingredients in a large mixing basin. Combine thoroughly.
4. Stuff each pattypan squash with the quinoa mixture, being sure to apply as little pressure as possible. If desired, vegan cheese can be sprinkled on top.
5. Cook the filled squash in a baking dish for forty to forty-five minutes or until the squash reaches the desired level of tenderness.
6. Immediately prior to serving, garnish with fresh parsley.

274.   VEGAN MARDI GRAS BRUSCHETTA

Total Time: 30 minutes

Prep Time: 15 minutes

Ingredients:

- 1 French baguette, sliced
- 1 cup cherry tomatoes, diced
- 1/2 cup red onion, finely chopped
- 1/4 cup fresh basil, chopped
- 2 tablespoons balsamic glaze

- 2 tablespoons olive oil
- Salt and pepper to taste
- 1 clove garlic, minced (for rubbing on the bread)

Directions:

1. Get the oven hot, about 175 degrees Celsius (350 degrees Fahrenheit).
2. The baguette slices should be arranged on a baking sheet and then toasted in the oven until they reach a golden brown color.
3. The tomatoes, red onion, basil, balsamic glaze, olive oil, salt, and pepper should be mixed together in a bowl by the cook. Combine thoroughly.
4. Garlic that has been minced should be rubbed into the toasted baguette pieces.
5. Place a dollop of the tomato stew on each individual piece.
6. Serve immediately as a lively appetizer for the Mardi Gras celebration.

275. CAJUN CAULIFLOWER BITES

Total Time: 40 minutes

Prep Time: 15 minutes

Ingredients:

- 1 head cauliflower, cut into florets
- 1 cup almond flour
- 1 cup unsweetened almond milk
- 1 cup breadcrumbs
- 2 tablespoons Cajun seasoning
- 1 teaspoon garlic powder
- Salt and pepper to taste
- Cooking spray

Directions:

1. Get your oven up to 425 °F (220 °C) before you start baking.
2. A batter may be made by combining almond flour, almond milk, Cajun spice, garlic powder, salt, and pepper in a single bowl.
3. Breadcrumbs should be placed in a separate bowl.
4. First, each cauliflower floret should be coated with breadcrumbs, and then it should be placed on a baking sheet after the batter coating.
5. A little coating of frying spray should be applied to the cauliflower.
6. Bake for twenty to twenty-five minutes or until well browned and crisp.
7. You may serve this with the vegan dipping sauce of your choice.

276. CREOLE-STYLE POTATO SALAD

Total Time: 45 minutes

Prep Time: 20 minutes

Ingredients:

- 4 cups red potatoes, boiled and diced
- 1/2 cup celery, finely chopped
- 1/4 cup red onion, finely chopped
- 1/4 cup pickles, diced
- 1/4 cup fresh parsley, chopped
- 1/2 cup vegan mayonnaise
- 2 tablespoons Dijon mustard
- 1 tablespoon Cajun seasoning
- Salt and pepper to taste

Directions:

1. Put the potatoes, celery, red onion, pickles, and parsley into a big bowl and mix them up properly.
2. In another bowl, mix together vegan mayonnaise, Dijon mustard, Cajun spice, salt, and pepper.
3. Apply the dressing to the potato mixture, then gently toss it so it is evenly coated with the dressing.
4. Before serving, place the dish in the refrigerator for at least half an hour to enable the flavors to combine.
5. Add some more chopped parsley as a garnish before serving.

277.   ZESTY OKRA ETOUFFEE

Total Time: 45 minutes

Prep Time: 15 minutes

Ingredients:

- 1 cup okra, sliced
- 1 onion, diced
- 1 bell pepper, chopped
- 2 celery stalks, diced
- 3 cloves garlic, minced
- 1 can diced tomatoes
- 1 cup vegetable broth
- 2 tablespoons tomato paste
- 1 teaspoon thyme
- 1 teaspoon paprika
- 1/2 teaspoon cayenne pepper
- Salt and pepper to taste
- 2 tablespoons oil
- Cooked rice for serving

Directions:

1. Boil the oil in a large pan over medium heat. Celery, onions, and bell peppers should be added. To soften the meat, sauté it.
2. After adding the garlic and okra, continue to simmer for another five minutes.
3. The tomatoes, tomato paste, vegetable broth, thyme, paprika, cayenne pepper, salt, and pepper should be stirred in at this point.
4. Until the flavors combine and the okra is soft, simmer for twenty to twenty-five minutes.
5. While the rice is cooking, serve.

278. VEGAN SHRIMP AND GRITS

Total Time: 40 minutes

Prep Time: 15 minutes

Ingredients:

- 1 cup grits
- 4 cups vegetable broth
- 1 cup vegan shrimp
- 1 onion, finely chopped
- 3 cloves garlic, minced
- 1 bell pepper, diced
- 1 cup cherry tomatoes, halved
- 1/2 cup vegan cheese, shredded
- 2 tablespoons nutritional yeast
- 2 tablespoons oil
- Salt and pepper to taste
- Fresh parsley for garnish

Directions:

1. Prepare the grits in accordance with the directions provided on the package, but use vegetable broth rather than water.
2. Sauté the onions, garlic, and bell pepper in a skillet until they have become more tender.
3. Put in some vegan shrimp, cherry tomatoes, and nutritional yeast, and season it with some salt and pepper. Prepare the shrimp until they are completely warm.
4. After the vegan cheese has melted and become creamy, mix it in.
5. After the grits have been cooked, serve the shrimp mixture on top of them, topped with fresh parsley.

279.   CAJUN POLENTA BITES

Total Time: 30 minutes

Prep Time: 10 minutes

Ingredients:

- 1 cup polenta
- 4 cups vegetable broth
- 1 tablespoon Cajun seasoning
- 1/2 cup vegan cream cheese
- 1/4 cup green onions, chopped
- 1/4 cup cherry tomatoes, diced
- Salt and pepper to taste
- Cooking spray

Directions:

1. Follow the package directions to cook the polenta in vegetable broth.
2. Mix together vegan cream cheese, green onions, cherry tomatoes, Cajun spice, a touch of pepper, and salt. Stir in the vegan dairy substitute.
3. Place the polenta on a skillet that has been oiled and spread it out evenly. Put in the refrigerator until it hardens.
4. Make bite-sized chunks out of the polenta that has been set.
5. The polenta bits should be pan-fried in a skillet that has been heated until they are brown on both sides.

280. CAJUN QUINOA BREAKFAST BOWL

Total Time: 25 minutes

Prep Time: 10 minutes

Ingredients:

- 1 cup quinoa, rinsed and drained
- 2 cups vegetable broth
- 1 tablespoon olive oil
- 1 onion, finely chopped
- 1 bell pepper, diced
- 2 cloves garlic, minced
- 1 teaspoon Cajun seasoning
- 1/2 teaspoon smoked paprika
- Salt and pepper to taste
- 1 cup cherry tomatoes, halved
- 1 cup black beans, cooked and drained
- 1 avocado, sliced
- Fresh parsley, chopped (for garnish)

Directions:

1. Quinoa and vegetable broth should be mixed together in a medium-sized pot. After a few minutes of boiling, lower the heat to low, cover, and simmer the quinoa for a further fifteen to twenty minutes, or until it is cooked through and the liquid is completely absorbed. Before putting it aside, fluff it with a fork.
2. Simmer the olive oil in a big saucepan over medium heat for a few minutes before using. For around five minutes, sauté the onions and bell peppers until they have become more tender.
3. In a pan, combine the following *Ingredients:* garlic, Cajun spice, smoked paprika, salt, and pepper. After stirring to mix, continue cooking for an additional two minutes.
4. To ensure that the quinoa is evenly coated with the Cajun seasoning combination, add cooked quinoa to the skillet and toss it thoroughly.
5. Add the cherry tomatoes and black beans, and continue to simmer for an additional three to four minutes until the mixture is completely heated.
6. Cajun quinoa combination should be served in bowls once it has been removed from the heat. The avocado should be sliced, and fresh parsley should be used as a garnish.
7. Delight in the delicious Cajun Quinoa Breakfast Bowl you've prepared!

281.   CAJUN QUINOA BREAKFAST BURRITOS

Total Time: 30 minutes

Prep Time: 15 minutes

Ingredients:

- 1 cup quinoa, cooked
- 1 cup black beans, drained and rinsed
- 1 cup corn kernels
- 1 red bell pepper, diced
- 1 onion, finely chopped
- 1 teaspoon Cajun seasoning
- 1 tablespoon olive oil
- Salt and pepper to taste
- 4 large whole wheat tortillas
- 1 avocado, sliced
- Fresh cilantro for garnish
- Salsa, for serving

Directions:

1. One way to get the olive oil ready is to heat it in a big pan over medium heat.
2. Sauté the onions and bell pepper till they have become more tender.
3. Cajun seasoning, quinoa that has been cooked, black beans, and corn should be added to the pan. Cook for a further five minutes after giving it a thorough stir.
4. After warming the tortillas, pour the quinoa mixture over each tortilla using a spoon.
5. On top, garnish with slices of avocado and cilantro. Use pepper and salt to season the food.
6. Burritos are created by rolling the tortillas into a roll. Ensure that salsa is served on the side.

282. CAJUN-STYLE VEGAN QUICHE

Total Time: 1 hour

Prep Time: 15 minutes

Ingredients:

- 1 pre-made vegan pie crust
- 1 cup firm tofu, crumbled
- 1 cup spinach, chopped
- 1 red bell pepper, diced
- 1 small zucchini, grated
- 1 cup unsweetened almond milk
- 2 tablespoons nutritional yeast
- 1 tablespoon Cajun seasoning
- Salt and pepper to taste

Directions:

1. Bring the oven up to a temperature of 375 F (190 C).
2. Put crumbled tofu, spinach, bell pepper, and zucchini into a bowl and mix them together.
3. In one dish, combine the almond milk, nutritional yeast, salt, pepper, and Cajun spice; stir to combine.
4. The wet mixture should be poured over the mixture of the tofu and vegetables. In order to mix, stir.
5. Once the mixture is in the pie crust, put it aside.
6. The quiche should be baked for forty to forty-five minutes or until it is set and golden brown.
7. Before slicing it, you should wait ten minutes for it to cool off.

283. VEGAN MARDI GRAS PASTA

Total Time: 45 minutes

Prep Time: 20 minutes

Ingredients:

- 8 oz fettuccine pasta
- 1 can (15 oz) diced tomatoes
- 1 cup bell peppers, sliced
- 1 cup okra, sliced
- 1 onion, diced
- 3 cloves garlic, minced
- 2 tablespoons Cajun seasoning
- 1 can (15 oz) black beans, drained and rinsed
- 2 tablespoons olive oil
- Salt and pepper to taste
- Fresh parsley, chopped (for garnish)

Directions:

1. Pasta should be cooked according to package recommendations. Drain, then keep away for later use.
2. One way to get the olive oil ready is to heat it in a big pan over medium heat. Okra, onions, and bell peppers should be added. To ensure that the veggies are cooked through.
3. Garlic, chopped tomatoes, Cajun spice, black beans, freshly ground black pepper, and salt should be added. Wait an extra five minutes before serving.
4. Once the pasta has been cooked, add it to the mixture and stir it thoroughly.
5. Immediately prior to serving, garnish with fresh parsley.

284.   VEGAN MARDI GRAS BISCUITS

Total Time: 30 minutes

Prep Time: 15 minutes

Ingredients:

- 2 cups all-purpose flour
- 1 tablespoon baking powder
- 1/2 teaspoon baking soda
- 1/2 teaspoon salt

- 1/2 cup vegan butter, cold and cubed
- 3/4 cup unsweetened almond milk
- 1 tablespoon apple cider vinegar
- 1 tablespoon Cajun seasoning

Directions:

1. Get your oven up to 425 °F (220 °C) before you start baking.
2. Blend the dry ingredients (flour, baking soda, baking powder, salt, and Cajun spice) in a bowl.
3. The mixture should be able to resemble coarse crumbs once the cold vegan butter has been cut in.
4. A separate dish should be used to combine the apple cider vinegar and almond milk. While stirring, add the wet liquid to the dry ingredients and ensure that they are just blended.
5. The dough should be turned out onto a surface that has been dusted with flour. Once the dough has reached a thickness of one inch, cut it into biscuits.
6. When the biscuits are just browned, about 12–15 minutes, transfer them to a baking sheet.

285. RED PEPPER AND ARTICHOKE BISQUE

Total Time: 45 minutes

Prep Time: 15 minutes

Serves: 4

Ingredients:

- 2 red bell peppers, roasted and peeled
- 1 can (14 oz) artichoke hearts, drained
- 1 onion, diced
- 3 cloves garlic, minced

- 1 tablespoon olive oil
- 4 cups vegetable broth
- 1 cup coconut milk
- 1 teaspoon Cajun seasoning
- Salt and pepper to taste
- Fresh parsley for garnish

Directions:

1. Coat the minced garlic and diced onion in olive oil and sauté in a large saucepan until they are soft.
2. When you add the artichoke hearts and roasted red peppers to the saucepan, make sure to stir them well.
3. After that, pour in the coconut milk and the vegetable broth. The mixture should be brought to a simmer.
4. Make sure the soup is completely smooth by blending it with an immersion blender.
5. Cajun seasoning, salt, and pepper need to be added to the dish. Adjust to your liking.
6. EnableSimmer for a further fifteen to twenty minutes to enable the flavors to combine.
7. Serve while still hot, with fresh parsley as a garnish.

286. VEGAN COLLARD GREEN WRAPS

Total Time: 30 minutes

Prep Time: 20 minutes

Serves: 2

Ingredients:

- 6 large collard green leaves
- 1 cup quinoa, cooked
- 1 cup black beans, cooked
- 1 cup corn kernels
- 1 cup cherry tomatoes, halved
- 1 avocado, sliced

- 1/4 cup red onion, finely chopped
- 2 tablespoons lime juice
- 2 tablespoons fresh cilantro, chopped
- Salt and pepper to taste

Directions:

1. Collard green leaves should be blanched in boiling water for one to two minutes, and then they should be submerged in freezing water. Dry with a towel.
2. Prepare the quinoa, black beans, corn, cherry tomatoes, red onion, lime juice, cilantro, salt, and pepper by combining all of the ingredients in a large bowl.
3. Position a leaf of collard greens on a surface that is level. The quinoa mixture should be spooned onto the middle part.
4. Wrap the collard leaf by first folding it in the sides of the leaf and then rolling it tightly to create a wrap.
5. Repeat with the remaining set of leaves.
6. Wraps should be cut in half before being served.

287.   VEGAN BAYOU BREAKFAST HASH

Total Time: 40 minutes

Prep Time: 15 minutes

Serves: 3-4

Ingredients:

- 2 tablespoons olive oil
- 1 onion, diced
- 2 bell peppers, diced
- 3 medium potatoes, diced
- 1 can (15 oz) black beans, drained and rinsed

- 1 teaspoon smoked paprika
- 1 teaspoon garlic powder
- 1/2 teaspoon cayenne pepper
- Salt and pepper to taste
- Fresh parsley for garnish

Directions:

1. The olive oil needs about 5 minutes to come to a boil in a large pan. The onions and bell peppers should be sautéed until they have become more tender.
2. The potatoes should be cooked until they are golden brown and crispy. Add the diced potatoes to the skillet.
3. Black beans, smoked paprika, garlic powder, cayenne pepper, salt, and pepper should be well combined and stirred together.
4. Ten to fifteen more minutes of cooking time will let the flavors blend.
5. Immediately prior to serving, garnish with fresh parsley.

288.   CAJUN THREE-BEAN SALAD

Total Time: 20 minutes

Prep Time: 15 minutes

Ingredients:

- 1 can (15 oz) black beans, drained and rinsed
- 1 can (15 oz) kidney beans, drained and rinsed
- 1 can (15 oz) chickpeas, drained and rinsed
- 1 cup corn kernels (fresh or frozen)
- 1/2 cup red bell pepper, diced
- 1/2 cup green bell pepper, diced
- 1/2 cup red onion, finely chopped
- 1/4 cup fresh cilantro, chopped
- For the Dressing:
- 1/4 cup olive oil
- 3 tablespoons red wine vinegar
- 1 tablespoon Cajun seasoning
- 1 teaspoon Dijon mustard
- Salt and pepper to taste

Directions:

1. In a large bowl, combine black beans, kidney beans, chickpeas, maize, red and green bell peppers, cilantro, red onion, and all the other ingredients.
2. Combine the olive oil, red wine vinegar, Cajun spice, Dijon mustard, salt, and pepper in a second, smaller bowl and whisk them together until they are thoroughly combined.
3. The dressing should be poured over the bean mixture and gently mixed to combine, making sure that all the ingredients are uniformly coated.
4. Ideally, you should marinate the salad in the fridge for half an hour before serving so the flavors can really jam.
5. This tasty Cajun Three-Bean Salad can be enjoyed as a light main course or as a refreshing side dish. Serve it cold.

289.   MUFFULETTA HUMMUS DIP

Total Time: 15 minutes

Prep Time: 10 minutes

Ingredients:

- 1 can (15 oz) chickpeas, drained and rinsed
- 1/4 cup tahini
- 3 tablespoons olive oil
- 2 cloves garlic, minced
- 2 tablespoons lemon juice
- 1 teaspoon Cajun seasoning
- 1/2 cup Kalamata olives, chopped
- 1/4 cup diced roasted red peppers
- 1/4 cup diced artichoke hearts
- Salt and pepper to taste
- Fresh parsley for garnish

Directions:

1. Put the chickpeas, tahini, olive oil, garlic, lemon juice, and Cajun spice into a food processor and pulse until everything is combined. Blend until it is completely smooth.
2. Transfer the hummus to a bowl used for serving, and then incorporate the artichoke hearts, chopped olives, and roasted red peppers into the hummus.
3. Before seasoning with salt, add pepper and salt to taste. For the garnish, combine some fresh parsley.
4. In addition to crackers, pita bread, or veggie sticks, serve this dish.

290. CAJUN CAULIFLOWER STEAK

Total Time: 40 minutes

Prep Time: 15 minutes

Ingredients:

- 1 large cauliflower head
- 3 tablespoons olive oil
- 2 tablespoons Cajun seasoning
- 1 teaspoon smoked paprika
- 1/2 teaspoon garlic powder
- Salt and pepper to taste
- Lemon wedges for serving

Directions:

1. Roast the vegetables until they are soft, about 20 minutes before serving.
2. Be sure to keep the core of the cauliflower intact when you remove the leaves and stem from it. The cauliflower should be cut into steaks that are one inch thick.
3. Olive oil, Cajun spice, smoked paprika, garlic powder, salt, and pepper should be combined in a small bowl and then stirred together.
4. Before placing the cauliflower steaks on a baking sheet, coat them on both sides with the spice mixture. Preheat the oven to 400 degrees.
5. Roast in an oven that has been warmed for twenty-five to thirty minutes or until the meat is golden brown and tender.
6. Hot, garnish with a squeezed lemon.

291.   SWEET POTATO AND CHICKPEA GUMBO

Total Time: 1 hour

Prep Time: 20 minutes

Ingredients:

- 2 tablespoons vegetable oil
- 1 onion, diced
- 2 bell peppers, diced
- 3 cloves garlic, minced
- 2 sweet potatoes, peeled and diced
- 1 can (15 oz) chickpeas, drained and rinsed
- 1 can (14 oz) diced tomatoes
- 4 cups vegetable broth
- 2 teaspoons Cajun seasoning
- 1 teaspoon thyme
- 1/2 teaspoon smoked paprika
- Salt and pepper to taste
- Cooked rice for serving

Directions:

1. In a large saucepan, bring the vegetable oil to a temperature of medium. The garlic, onion, and bell peppers should be added. To soften the meat, sauté it.
2. Cajun seasoning, smoked paprika, thyme, sweet potatoes, chickpeas, chopped tomatoes, vegetable broth, and salt and pepper are the ingredients that should be included.
3. Continue boiling the sweet potatoes for a further forty minutes after the mixture has reached a boil. Maintain the sweet potatoes' cooking by lowering the heat to a simmer and continuing to cook them. To taste, adjust the spice and serve over rice that has been cooked.

292. VEGAN HUSHPUPPIES

Total Time: 25 minutes

Prep Time: 15 minutes

Ingredients:

- 1 cup cornmeal
- 1/2 cup all-purpose flour
- 1 teaspoon baking powder
- 1/2 teaspoon baking soda
- 1/2 teaspoon Cajun seasoning
- 1/2 cup finely chopped green onions
- 1/2 cup corn kernels
- 1 tablespoon flaxseed meal + 3 tablespoons water (flax egg)
- 1 cup non-dairy milk
- Vegetable oil for frying

Directions:

1. Flour, cornmeal, baking soda, baking powder, and Cajun seasoning should all be mixed together in a basin. Mix up the ingredients until they are evenly distributed.
2. A flax egg may be made by combining flaxseed grain and water in a separate bowl. Blend in the non-dairy milk after adding it.
3. After adding the liquid components to the dry ones, stir the mixture until it is almost completely incorporated. The corn kernels and green onions should be folded in.
4. The vegetable oil should be heated to 350 degrees Fahrenheit (180 degrees Celsius) in a deep skillet.
5. To cook the batter, heat the oil and put spoonfuls into it. Cook, flipping often, until golden.
6. Using a slotted spoon, remove the food and set it on paper towels to allow any leftover oil to drain.
7. Top with your preferred dipping sauce and serve while still hot.

293. SWEET POTATO AND BLACK BEAN GRITS

Total Time: 30 minutes

Prep Time: 10 minutes

Ingredients:

- 1 cup stone-ground grits
- 2 cups water
- 1 cup unsweetened almond milk
- 1 large sweet potato, peeled and diced
- 1 can black beans, drained and rinsed
- 1 tablespoon Cajun seasoning
- Salt and pepper to taste
- 2 tablespoons vegan butter
- Fresh chives for garnish

Directions:

1. Heat the almond milk and water in a pot until they boil, stirring regularly. Take the skillet from the stove and mix in the grits. To thicken the mixture, reduce heat to low and simmer, stirring often, for around fifteen to twenty minutes.
2. Prepare the sweet potato by steaming it until it is delicate enough to pierce with a fork.
3. Sweet potato, black beans, Cajun spice, salt, and pepper should be mixed together in a separate pan or skillet. Once everything is thoroughly blended and heated up, sauté it.
4. Incorporate the vegan butter into the cooked grits and stir until melted. If it is required, adjust the seasoning.
5. It is recommended that the sweet potato and black bean combination be served on top of the grits. Serve with a garnish of fresh chives.

294.   VEGAN MUFFULETTA PANINI

Total Time: 15 minutes

Prep Time: 5 minutes

Ingredients:

- 1 round vegan muffuletta bread
- 1/2 cup vegan olive tapenade
- 1/2 cup marinated artichoke hearts, chopped
- 1/2 cup roasted red peppers, sliced
- 1/2 cup vegan mozzarella, shredded
- 1 tablespoon olive oil for grilling

Directions:

1. Start by preheating a grill pan or a panini press.
2. The bread for the muffuletta should be cut horizontally. On one side of the bread, spread olive tapenade across the surface.
3. To finish off the tapenade, arrange artichoke hearts, roasted red peppers, and vegan mozzarella in a layering pattern.
4. In order to make a sandwich, place the other half of the bread on top of the first half.
5. Olive oil should be used to coat the exterior of the sandwich, and then it should be grilled until the bread is lightly browned and the filling is warm and melted.

295.   CAJUN CHICKPEA STEW

Total Time: 40 minutes

Prep Time: 15 minutes

Ingredients:

- 2 cans chickpeas, drained and rinsed
- 1 onion, finely chopped
- 3 cloves garlic, minced
- 1 bell pepper, diced
- 1 celery stalk, chopped
- 1 can diced tomatoes

- 2 cups vegetable broth
- 1 tablespoon Cajun seasoning
- 1 teaspoon thyme
- Salt and pepper to taste
- 2 tablespoons olive oil
- Cooked rice for serving

Directions:

1. A large pot should be heated at a medium temperature with the olive oil. To the pan, add the celery, onions, garlic, and bell pepper. For veggies to become more tender, sauté them.
2. The chickpeas, chopped tomatoes, vegetable broth, Cajun spice, thyme, salt, and pepper should be stirred in at this point. Allow to come to a simmer.
3. Put the stew over low heat and let it simmer for twenty to twenty-five minutes. This will allow the flavors to combine.
4. On top of the rice that has been cooked, serve the Cajun chickpea stew.

296. CAJUN SWEET POTATO HASH

Total Time: 35 minutes

Prep Time: 10 minutes

Ingredients:

- 2 large sweet potatoes, peeled and diced
- 1 onion, diced
- 1 bell pepper, diced
- 2 cloves garlic, minced

- 2 tablespoons olive oil
- 1 tablespoon Cajun seasoning
- Salt and pepper to taste
- Fresh parsley for garnish

Directions:

1. One way to get the olive oil ready is to heat it in a big pan over medium heat. Include garlic, sweet potatoes, onion, and bell pepper in the dish.
2. On top of the veggies, sprinkle some Cajun spice, along with some salt and pepper. To ensure a uniform coating, stir.
3. Make sure to toss the sweet potatoes regularly while they are cooking for twenty to twenty-five minutes.
4. Immediately prior to serving, garnish with fresh parsley.

297.   VEGAN JAMBALAYA-STUFFED BELL PEPPERS

Total Time: 1 hour 15 minutes

Prep Time: 30 minutes

Ingredients:

- 4 large bell peppers, halved and seeds removed
- 1 cup brown rice, cooked
- 1 cup vegan sausage, diced
- 1 cup okra, sliced
- 1 cup diced tomatoes
- 1 onion, finely chopped
- 3 cloves garlic, minced
- 1 tablespoon Cajun seasoning
- 1 teaspoon smoked paprika
- 1 teaspoon thyme
- Salt and pepper to taste
- 2 cups vegetable broth
- 2 tablespoons olive oil
- Fresh parsley for garnish

Directions:

1. Get the oven hot, about 190 degrees Celsius (375 degrees Fahrenheit).
2. Get the olive oil ready by warming it in a large saucepan over medium heat. Onions and garlic should be sautéed until more tender.
3. Cajun seasoning, smoked paprika, thyme, salt, and pepper should be added to the mixture, along with vegan sausage, okra, and tomatoes, 5-7 minutes of cooking time.
4. The cooked rice and veggie broth should be stirred in. Let the mixture continue to simmer for another five to seven minutes.
5. In a baking dish, arrange the bell pepper halves in a cluster. To fill each pepper, place a spoonful of the jambalaya mixture.
6. Bake the casserole with the foil covering it for thirty to thirty-five minutes or until the peppers are soft.
7. Immediately prior to serving, garnish with fresh parsley.

298.   CAJUN-STYLE VEGAN BLACK-EYED PEA SALAD

Total Time: 15 minutes

Prep Time: 15 minutes

Ingredients:

- 2 cans (15 oz each) of black-eyed peas, drained and rinsed
- 1 cup corn kernels, fresh or frozen
- 1 bell pepper, diced
- 1/2 red onion, finely chopped
- 1 celery stalk, finely sliced
- 1/4 cup fresh parsley, chopped
- 2 tablespoons olive oil
- 2 tablespoons apple cider vinegar
- 1 tablespoon Cajun seasoning
- Salt and pepper to taste
- Lemon wedges for serving

Directions:

1. Black-eyed peas, corn, bell pepper, red onion, celery, and parsley should be mixed together in a big basin.
2. Olive oil, apple cider vinegar, Cajun spice, salt, and pepper should be mixed together in a small bowl after being whisked together.
3. Apply the dressing to the salad, then toss it to ensure that it is uniformly coated.
4. Before serving, place in the refrigerator for at least one hour.
5. Lemon wedges should be used as a garnish when serving cold.

299. CAJUN QUINOA STUFFED TOMATOES

Total Time: 45 minutes

Prep Time: 20 minutes

Ingredients:

- 6 large tomatoes, tops removed and insides scooped out
- 1 cup quinoa, cooked
- 1 cup black beans, cooked
- 1 cup corn kernels, fresh or frozen
- 1 bell pepper, diced
- 1/2 red onion, finely chopped
- 2 cloves garlic, minced
- 1 tablespoon Cajun seasoning
- 1 teaspoon cumin
- 1/4 cup fresh cilantro, chopped
- 2 tablespoons lime juice
- Salt and pepper to taste
- Avocado slices for serving

Directions:

1. Set the oven temperature to 190 degrees Celsius (375 degrees Fahrenheit).
2. All of the following ingredients should be combined in a big bowl: cooked quinoa, black beans, corn, bell pepper, red onion, garlic, Cajun spice, cumin, cilantro, lime juice, salt, and pepper.
3. Apply the quinoa mixture to the inside of each tomato, and then set the tomatoes in a baking dish.
4. Bake the tomatoes for twenty to twenty-five minutes or until they are soft.
5. Add slices of avocado to the top of the dish.

300. CAJUN CORN AND SWEET POTATO CHOWDER

Total Time: 50 minutes

Prep Time: 15 minutes

Ingredients:

- 2 tablespoons olive oil
- 1 onion, diced
- 2 cloves garlic, minced
- 2 sweet potatoes, peeled and diced
- 1 bell pepper, diced
- 1 celery stalk, diced
- 1 teaspoon Cajun seasoning
- 1/2 teaspoon smoked paprika
- 4 cups vegetable broth
- 2 cups corn kernels, fresh or frozen
- 1 cup coconut milk
- Salt and pepper to taste
- Green onions for garnish

Directions:

1. In a large saucepan, brown the olive oil over medium heat.
2. To create a fragrant aroma, sauté the onions and garlic.
3. Include smoked paprika, sweet potatoes, bell peppers, and celery in the dish, along with Cajun flavor. 5-7 minutes of cooking time.
4. Once the vegetable broth has been added, bring the mixture to a boil.
5. Keep cooking the sweet potatoes, reducing heat as needed, until they reach a soft consistency.
6. Mix with some maize and coconut milk. Continuing to simmer for another ten to fifteen minutes.
7. Use pepper and salt to season the food. Green onions should be used as a garnish before serving.

301.   SPICY CAJUN CHICKPEA STEW

Total Time: 45 minutes

Prep Time: 15 minutes

Ingredients:

- 2 cans (15 oz each) chickpeas, drained and rinsed
- 1 tablespoon olive oil
- 1 onion, diced
- 3 cloves garlic, minced
- 1 bell pepper, diced
- 2 celery stalks, chopped
- 1 can (14 oz) diced tomatoes
- 1 cup vegetable broth
- 1 teaspoon Cajun seasoning
- 1/2 teaspoon paprika
- 1/4 teaspoon cayenne pepper (adjust to taste)
- Salt and pepper to taste
- Fresh parsley for garnish

Directions:

1. In a large saucepan, brown the olive oil over medium heat.
2. To the pan, add the celery, onions, garlic, and bell pepper. To ensure that the veggies are cooked through.
3. Chickpeas, chopped tomatoes, vegetable broth, Cajun spice, paprika, and cayenne pepper should be added to the ingredients. Give it a good stir.
4. Stir the stew until it reaches a simmer, then allow it to cook for twenty-five to thirty minutes so that the flavors may combine.
5. Before seasoning with salt, add pepper and salt to taste. Add a sprig of fresh parsley just before serving.
6. The piping hot meal goes well with rice or crunchy bread.

302. VEGAN OKRA CORNBREAD MUFFINS

Total Time: 30 minutes

Prep Time: 10 minutes

Ingredients:

- 1 cup cornmeal
- 1 cup all-purpose flour
- 1 tablespoon baking powder
- 1/2 teaspoon salt

- 1 cup almond milk (or any plant-based milk)
- 1/4 cup maple syrup
- 1/4 cup vegetable oil
- 1 cup frozen okra, chopped

Directions:

1. Roast the vegetables until they are soft, about 20 minutes before serving. Use paper liners or a muffin tray that has been greased.
2. The cornmeal, flour, baking powder, and salt should be mixed together in a large basin using a whisk.
3. In a separate dish, mix together the maple syrup, vegetable oil, and almond milk before proceeding.
4. After adding the liquid components to the dry ones, stir the mixture until it is almost completely incorporated. Add the chopped okra and fold it in.
5. Apply the batter to the muffin cups using a spoon, filling each one approximately two-thirds of the way.
6. After inserting a toothpick into the middle of the cake, bake it for 18 to 20 minutes or until it comes out clean.
7. After allowing the muffins to cool for a few minutes, move them to a wire rack to finish cooling.

303.   MUFFULETTA FLATBREAD PIZZA

Total Time: 25 minutes

Prep Time: 10 minutes

Ingredients:

- 2 flatbreads
- 1/2 cup vegan Muffuletta olive salad
- 1 cup cherry tomatoes, halved
- 1/2 cup marinated artichoke hearts, chopped
- 1/4 cup sliced black olives
- 1/4 cup sliced green olives
- 1 cup vegan mozzarella cheese, shredded
- Fresh basil for garnish

Directions:

1. Get your oven up to 425 °F (220 °C) before you start baking.
2. A baking sheet should be used to place the flatbreads. Distribute a substantial amount of Muffuletta olive salad on top of each individual flatbread.
3. On top of the flatbreads, distribute cherry tomatoes, artichoke hearts, black olives, and green olives in an even manner.
4. The vegan mozzarella cheese should be sprinkled on top. The pizza needs around 12–15 minutes in a preheated oven to melt the cheese and get some browning on the edges.
5. The dish should be removed from the oven and topped with fresh basil before being served.

304. VEGAN MUFFULETTA FLATBREAD PIZZA

Total Time: 25 minutes

Prep Time: 10 minutes

Ingredients:

- 2 flatbreads
- 1/2 cup vegan Muffuletta olive salad
- 1 cup cherry tomatoes, halved
- 1/2 cup marinated artichoke hearts, chopped
- 1/4 cup sliced black olives
- 1/4 cup sliced green olives
- 1 cup vegan mozzarella cheese, shredded
- Fresh basil for garnish

Directions:

1. Get your oven up to 425 °F (220 °C) before you start baking.
2. A baking sheet should be used to place the flatbreads. Distribute a substantial amount of vegan Muffuletta olive salad on top of each individual flatbread.
3. On top of the flatbreads, distribute cherry tomatoes, artichoke hearts, black olives, and green olives in an even manner.
4. The vegan mozzarella cheese should be sprinkled on top.
5. The pizza needs around 12–15 minutes in a preheated oven to melt the cheese and get some browning on the edges.
6. The dish should be removed from the oven and topped with fresh basil before being served.

305. VEGAN CREOLE STUFFED BELL PEPPERS

Total Time: 1 hour 30 minutes

Prep Time: 30 minutes

Ingredients:

- 4 large bell peppers, halved and seeds removed
- 1 cup quinoa, cooked
- 1 can (15 oz) black beans, drained and rinsed
- 1 cup corn kernels (fresh or frozen)
- 1 cup diced tomatoes
- 1 cup diced onion
- 2 cloves garlic, minced
- 1 tablespoon Cajun seasoning
- Salt and pepper to taste
- 1 cup tomato sauce
- 1 cup vegan shredded cheese

Directions:

1. Set the oven temperature to 190 degrees Celsius (375 degrees Fahrenheit).
2. Combine the quinoa that has been cooked, the black beans, the corn, the tomatoes, the onion, the garlic, the Cajun spice, the salt, and the pepper in a large mixing bowl.
3. Prepare a baking dish and fill each half of a bell pepper with the quinoa mixture. Place the peppers in the dish.
4. Once the peppers have been packed, pour tomato sauce over them and then top them with vegan shredded cheese.
5. Bake for forty-five minutes with the baking dish covered with aluminum foil. If you like tender peppers and bubbling cheese, bake for another fifteen minutes; if not, bake for a little longer.
6. Remove the foil and continue baking.
7. Take the dish out of the oven, allow it to have a few minutes to cool, and then serve.

306.   VEGAN HUSHPUPPY WAFFLES

Total Time: 25 minutes

Prep Time: 10 minutes

Ingredients:

- 2 cups cornmeal
- 1 cup all-purpose flour
- 2 teaspoons baking powder
- 1 teaspoon baking soda
- 1 teaspoon salt
- 1 cup corn kernels (fresh or frozen)

- 1 cup finely chopped green onions
- 1 ½ cups non-dairy milk
- ¼ cup vegetable oil
- 2 tablespoons maple syrup
- 1 tablespoon apple cider vinegar

Directions:

1. The waffle iron should be preheated in accordance with the recommendations provided by the manufacturer.
2. To whip up the batter, in a large basin, whisk together the cornmeal, flour, baking powder, baking soda, and salt.
3. The dry components should be supplemented with corn kernels and green onions.
4. In a separate dish, whisk together the non-dairy milk, vegetable oil, maple syrup, and apple cider vinegar.
5. After adding the liquid components to the dry ones, stir the mixture until it is almost completely incorporated.
6. Place batter on the waffle iron that has been preheated, and then cook it in accordance with the directions provided by the manufacturer.
7. With the vegan toppings of your choice, serve the hushpuppy waffles while they are still warm.

307. MUFFULETTA PASTA SALAD

Total Time: 20 minutes

Prep Time: 10 minutes

Ingredients:

- 8 oz rotini pasta, cooked and cooled
- 1 cup mixed olives, chopped
- 1 cup cherry tomatoes, halved
- 1 cup diced bell peppers (red and green)
- 1 cup artichoke hearts, chopped
- 1 cup vegan mozzarella cheese, cubed
- ½ cup sliced red onion
- ½ cup fresh parsley, chopped

Directions:

1. All of the following ingredients should be mixed together in a big bowl: cooked pasta, olives, cherry tomatoes, bell peppers, artichoke hearts, vegan mozzarella, red onion, and parsley.
2. Use a tossing motion to thoroughly incorporate all of the ingredients.
3. After tossing the salad once again, proceed to drizzle your preferred vinaigrette or olive oil over it.
4. A minimum of one hour should be spent chilling the pasta salad in the refrigerator before it is served.
5. Take pleasure in the taste of a traditional muffuletta in the shape of pasta salad when you serve it cold.

308.   CAJUN COLLARD GREEN SPRING ROLLS

Total Time: 45 minutes

Prep Time: 25 minutes

Ingredients:

- 8 large collard green leaves, stems removed
- 1 cup cooked quinoa
- 1 cup blackened Cajun tofu, diced
- 1 cup shredded carrots
- 1 cup cucumber, julienned
- 1 avocado, sliced
- ½ cup fresh cilantro leaves
- ¼ cup roasted peanuts, chopped
- Rice paper wrappers

Directions:

1. By blanching the collard green leaves in boiling water for one to two minutes until they become pliable, you may prepare them. A paper towel should be used to pat them dry.
2. When you have a clean surface, lay a collard green leaf down flat. In the middle of the leaf, place a tiny amount of quinoa, Cajun tofu, shredded carrots, cucumber, avocado, cilantro, and peanuts. Repeat with the other ingredients.
3. Using a technique similar to that of a burrito, fold the edges of the collard green inward and then roll it up securely.
4. Repeat the process with the other ingredients and the leaves of the collard green.
5. Please prepare the rice paper wrappers in accordance with the directions provided on the box.
6. Prepare the Cajun collard green spring rolls and serve them with the dipping sauce of your preference.

309.   VEGAN ZYDECO POTATO SALAD

Total Time: 30 minutes

Prep Time: 15 minutes

Ingredients:

- 4 cups baby potatoes, boiled and diced
- 1/2 cup celery, finely chopped
- 1/4 cup red onion, finely chopped
- 1/4 cup pickles, diced
- 1/4 cup fresh parsley, chopped
- 1/2 cup vegan mayonnaise
- 1 tablespoon Dijon mustard
- 1 tablespoon apple cider vinegar
- Salt and pepper to taste
- Cajun seasoning for an extra kick (optional)

Directions:

1. Put the diced potatoes, celery, red onion, pickles, and parsley into a large bowl and mix those ingredients together.
2. Combine the vegan mayonnaise, Dijon mustard, apple cider vinegar, salt, pepper, and Cajun seasoning in a separate bowl and whisk together until smooth. If preferred, add Cajun seasoning.
3. Gently toss the potato mixture after pouring the dressing over it until everything is thoroughly mixed.
4. Before serving, place the dish in the refrigerator for at least fifteen minutes to allow the flavors to combine.
5. The dish should be served cold and garnished with extra parsley. Your Vegan Zydeco Potato Salad is waiting for you!

310.   CAJUN COLLARD GREEN QUESADILLAS

Total Time: 40 minutes

Prep Time: 20 minutes

Ingredients:

- 8 large collard green leaves, stems removed
- 1 cup black beans, cooked
- 1 cup corn kernels
- 1 cup red bell pepper, diced

- 1 cup vegan cheese, shredded
- 1 teaspoon Cajun seasoning
- 1 tablespoon olive oil
- Whole wheat or corn tortillas

Directions:

1. Make sure to blanch the collard green leaves for two minutes in water that is boiling. Remove, and then use a paper towel to dry the area gently.
2. Cajun seasoning should be used to sauté black beans, corn, and red bell pepper along with olive oil in a pan until the vegetables are soft.
3. The collard green leaves should be laid out, and the sautéed mixture should be distributed among them.
4. On top of each collard leaf, sprinkle vegan cheese, then fold the leaf in a manner similar to a quesadilla.
5. In a pan, put the collard greens that have been folded and heat them until the cheese has melted and the leaves have become crisp.
6. Serve hot, sliced into wedges, and as desired. Be sure to savor your Quesadillas with Cajun Collard Green!

311.　SPICY CORN MAQUE CHOUX

Total Time: 35 minutes

Prep Time: 15 minutes

Ingredients:

- 2 cups fresh or frozen corn kernels
- 1 cup bell peppers (mix of red and green), diced
- 1 cup tomatoes, diced
- 1/2 cup onion, finely chopped
- 2 cloves garlic, minced
- 1 teaspoon Cajun seasoning
- 1/4 teaspoon cayenne pepper (adjust to taste)
- 2 tablespoons olive oil
- Fresh parsley for garnish

Directions:

1. Get the olive oil ready by warming it in a skillet over medium heat. As soon as the onions and garlic become transparent, add them.
2. Include corn, tomatoes, and bell peppers in the dish. You should cook the veggies until they are soft.
3. Include cayenne pepper and Cajun seasoning in the seasoning mix. Make the necessary adjustments to the degree of heat to suit your tastes.
4. Continue to cook for a further five minutes, stirring the mixture each time.
5. Serve when hot and garnish with chopped fresh parsley. Indulge in some of your Spicy Corn Maque Choux!

312. MARDI GRAS QUINOA CAKES

Total Time: 45 minutes

Prep Time: 20 minutes

Ingredients:

- 1 cup quinoa, cooked and cooled
- 1 cup black beans, mashed
- 1/2 cup bell peppers (any color), finely diced
- 1/4 cup red onion, finely chopped
- 2 cloves garlic, minced
- 2 tablespoons Cajun seasoning
- 1/4 cup breadcrumbs
- 2 tablespoons flaxseed meal + 6 tablespoons water (flax eggs)
- Olive oil for frying

Directions:

1. The following ingredients should be mixed together in a big bowl: quinoa, mashed black beans, bell peppers, red onion, garlic, Cajun spice, breadcrumbs, and flax eggs.
2. After thoroughly combining the mix, you may alter the mixture's consistency by adding more breadcrumbs if needed.
3. After shaping the mixture into patties, lay them on a dish that has been lined with parchment paper.
4. Get the olive oil heated up to medium-high in a skillet. Fry the quinoa cakes until they are golden brown on both sides.
5. While it's still hot, serve with your favorite dipping sauce.
6. Have fun eating your Quinoa Cakes for Mardi Gras!

313. VEGAN CAJUN CAESAR SALAD

Total Time: 20 minutes

Prep Time: 10 minutes

Servings: 4

Ingredients:

- 1 head of romaine lettuce, chopped
- 1 cup cherry tomatoes, halved
- 1 cup croutons
- 1/2 cup vegan Caesar dressing
- 1/4 cup nutritional yeast
- 1/4 cup capers
- Cajun seasoning to taste
- Lemon wedges for garnish

Directions:

1. Salad ingredients include romaine lettuce, cherry tomatoes, and croutons, all diced and placed in a large dish.
2. After drizzling vegan Caesar dressing over the salad, toss it to ensure that it is uniformly coated.
3. To finish off the salad, sprinkle some nutritional yeast and capers on top.
4. Cajun seasoning should be added to taste and adjusted accordingly.
5. Lemon wedges should be used as a garnish and served immediately.

314.   CAJUN-STYLE VEGAN CABBAGE ROLLS

Total Time: 1 hour 30 minutes

Prep Time: 30 minutes

Cook Time: 1 hour

Servings: 6

Ingredients:

- 12 large cabbage leaves, blanched
- 1 cup quinoa, cooked
- 1 can black beans, drained and rinsed
- 1 cup diced tomatoes
- 1 onion, finely chopped
- 2 cloves garlic, minced
- 1 tablespoon Cajun seasoning
- 1 cup tomato sauce
- Salt and pepper to taste
- Chopped green onions for garnish

Directions:

1. Get the oven hot, about 175 degrees Celsius (350 degrees Fahrenheit).
2. Combine the quinoa that has been cooked, the black beans, the diced tomatoes, the onion, the garlic, and the Cajun spice in a large bowl.
3. A teaspoon of the mixture should be placed on each cabbage leaf, and then the leaf should be securely rolled.
4. Using a baking dish, arrange the cabbage rolls in a formation.
5. On top of the rolls, drizzle some tomato sauce, and then season them with salt and pepper.
6. Bake for one hour with the foil covering the dish.
7. Prior to serving, garnish with green onions that have been chopped.

315. SAVORY CORN MAQUE CHOUX

Total Time: 40 minutes

Prep Time: 15 minutes

Cook Time: 25 minutes

Servings: 4

Ingredients:

- 4 cups fresh or frozen corn kernels
- 1 bell pepper, diced
- 1 onion, diced
- 2 cloves garlic, minced
- 1 cup cherry tomatoes, halved
- 1 teaspoon Cajun seasoning
- 1/2 teaspoon smoked paprika
- 1/4 cup chopped fresh parsley
- Salt and pepper to taste

Directions:

1. Sauté the onion and bell pepper in a large pan until they have become more tender.
2. After adding the garlic, continue to simmer for one more minute.
3. Corn, cherry tomatoes, Cajun spice, and smoked paprika should be stirred in at this point.
4. Keep cooking for fifteen to twenty minutes or until the veggies are soft.
5. Before seasoning with salt, add pepper and salt to taste.
6. Before serving, garnish with chopped parsley from the garden.

316.   CABBAGE AND PECAN SLAW

Total Time: 15 minutes

Prep Time: 10 minutes

Servings: 6

Ingredients:

- 1/2 head green cabbage, thinly sliced
- 1/2 cup pecans, chopped
- 1/4 cup raisins
- 1/4 cup vegan mayonnaise
- 2 tablespoons Dijon mustard
- 1 tablespoon apple cider vinegar
- 1 tablespoon maple syrup
- Salt and pepper to taste
- Fresh parsley for garnish

Directions:

1. Put the sliced cabbage, pecans, and raisins into a big bowl and mix them well.
2. Vegan mayonnaise, Dijon mustard, apple cider vinegar, and maple syrup should be mixed together in a small basin.
3. Coat the cabbage mixture evenly by pouring the dressing over it and tossing.
4. Before seasoning with salt, add pepper and salt to taste.
5. Immediately prior to serving, garnish with fresh parsley.

THE END

Made in the USA
Monee, IL
01 June 2025

18553622R10179